Lenten Prayers for Busy People

Lenten Prayers
for Busy People

*A Forty-Day Retreat
Wherever You Happen to Be*

William J. O'Malley

ORBIS BOOKS

Maryknoll, New York 10545

Founded in 1970, Orbis Books endeavors to publish works that enlighten the mind, nourish the spirit, and challenge the conscience. The publishing arm of the Maryknoll Fathers and Brothers, Orbis seeks to explore the global dimensions of the Christian faith and mission, to invite dialogue with diverse cultures and religious traditions, and to serve the cause of reconciliation and peace. The books published reflect the views of their authors and do not represent the official position of the Maryknoll Society. To learn more about Maryknoll and Orbis Books, please visit our website at www.maryknoll.org.

Manufactured in the United States of America.
Manuscript editing and typesetting by Joan Weber Laflamme.

Library of Congress Cataloging-in-Publication Data

O'Malley, William J.
   Lenten prayers for busy people : a forty-day retreat wherever you happen to be / William J. O'Malley.
      p. cm.
   ISBN 1-57075-562-0 (pbk.)
   1. Lent—Prayer-books and devotions—English. I. Title.
   BV85.O48 2004
   242'.34—dc22

                                    2004006510

This book
is for
Pat and Dick Rohrer

Contents

Felt Remembrance

Sometimes I wish I were a Jew. It seems they have a sense of sacred symbolic history branded into their very fibers from birth. Even those who don't practice seem to feel it on the holy days: a communally *felt remembrance*. It is as if they themselves (or at the very least their grandparents) had actually followed the great Moses through the Red Sea and across the hostile desert to the Promised Land, underwent the shame of the captivity and the exhilaration of the return, bore within their own souls the scars of thirty centuries of humiliation.

I did feel that once, about our common, sacred Christian memories—the nativity, the crucifixion, the resurrection—for the first three decades of my life, along with so many others raised in a near-ghetto Catholicism. The Latin, the Ember and Rogation days (which today few Catholics could even explain), the strict Lenten and Advent fasts (not to mention the scrupulous fast before receiving communion), novenas and parish missions, the realization that if our sins were of no importance, we ourselves were of no importance. And if we older selves can't muster a felt remembrance of a simpler, more "enchanted" past whose symbols enabled us to *feel* Catholic, an experience we *did* actually live through, it is surely unfair to expect it of those under forty who never experienced *feeling* Catholic, or, more profoundly, to expect that the very young, the future Church, will experience within themselves the *sacred importance* of the trans-historical events we celebrated during

Advent and Lent: the nativity, the crucifixion, the resurrection.

I truly miss that.

When I was finally allowed to think about my Christian beliefs rationally (which didn't begin until I was thirty-two), my sense of the *feeling* of Christian practice began to ebb away. I do still feel it, nearly always and sometimes palpably, at the consecration, but not at Lent or Advent or any of the feasts that used to have such a savory holy importance. Now Advent and Lent seem, at least to me, an attempt to fake a feeling of breathless expectation, on the one hand, and of cumulative dread, on the other.

Part of the change, to be sure, has been due to the iconoclasm that followed Vatican II. Historical correctness, cerebralizing, and sophistication banished all the mystery and enchantment. Educated Catholics (and thus their children) began to feel almost embarrassed by credulous belief in the efficacy of symbols like the rosary or lighting a candle at Our Lady's shrine or wearing a crucifix (except as a kind of macho "jewelry"). The tabernacle (with its truly present "prisoner" Host) was shunted to the side somewhere. Statues of saints were stowed away, like our doll houses and baseball mitts, and replaced by sleek non-representational artifacts. Emphasis at the liturgy was refocused from the Host to the community, which very often existed only in the minds of liturgists. A few parishes burgeoned into vibrant new life; many did not.

Thinking didn't help, either, when I realized Jesus had told us, when we fast, we should *not* put ashes on our heads, and yet we had institutionalized what he forbade. Ironically, though, ashes—and the palms from which they came—remained two of the few symbols that stayed potent and meaningful for most Catholics after all the iconoclasm. A puzzlement. A rebellion of the intuitive heart against the critical mind.

To be truthful, I also resisted the fact that the liturgists had now made such "opportunities" as an Easter Midnight Mass that grinds on for three whole hours, readings upon readings that had meaning only for them. And if a hymn has ten verses, we must "get through" all ten.

Another part of the reason for the disenchantment was a series of events in the middle of the last century—World War II, the G.I. Bill, the booming economy, Fulton Sheen, Jack Kennedy—that moved Catholics into the mainstream. But you can't blend in without being diluted. Many symbols and practices that made "us" became less meaningful than being accepted by "them."

Part of the drain on my "feeling Catholic" is also rooted in the fact I've been teaching apologetics to boys for over forty years. There's no room for feelings in apologetics, not when the challenges are "The Bible is nothing but a lot of made-up stories," and "If the Vatican is so stupid about artificial birth control for lifelong committed couples, what does it know about anything else?" and "C'mon! If she wants it as much as you do, who's getting hurt?" To face those truculent objections, one needs the skills of Professor Harold Hill, not those of Teresa of Avila. Skepticism isn't short-circuited by taking a nature walk and asking, "Can you *feel* the aliveness in the wind? Can you *sense* the presence of Someone lurking, full of energizing power, under the skins of everything we see and touch?" (At least not after early grade school, where it never happens either. The teachers are too busy teaching the mandated doctrines the kids care nothing about and are incapable of understanding in the first place.)

That's probably a core reason of my disenchantment: I was finally encouraged to *think*. to open the iron door between my left brain, where I stored my seven years of Thomistic philosophy and theology, and my right brain where I kept all my deepest and most life-giving beliefs. It was shocking to find that those who wrote the gospels weren't eyewitnesses, that snakes never tried to sell fruit to naked ladies in the park, that Jesus probably never walked on water—and yet that it was all still truth bearing, non-historical but still full of meaning.

At that extreme of rationalism we forget, in our innocent arrogance, that—for all our *Summas* and catechisms, our centuries of ecumenical councils with their *homoousios* and *filioque*, we are faced with a Being whose self-definition is only "I AM," that the profoundest of theologians is no closer to comprehending or circumscribing God than an old lady running her beads through her wrinkled fingers in a (seemingly) empty church.

What all of us lost in all that head-tripping and liturgical revision was the root of *religion—religare*—"to bind together tightly," that is, the person-to-Person connection with God.

But the core of my resistance to faking an expectation during Advent and a gloomy dread during Lent was sublimely ironic. Despite—or perhaps because of—all the tailspins and changes, the disenchantments and demythologizing of my peasant faith, I was finally forced to wrestle within my soul for what I *really* believed. And I found that I really believed—and trusted—in the resurrection of Jesus. No one witnessed it (and if the evangelists wanted to fake it, they *could* have included a nifty Spielberg resurrection scene—but they didn't). The "proof" we have that Jesus actually survived death is that the disciples who were abject cowards on Good Friday became fearless preachers within a couple of months of their despair. They said the change came about because of their certain encounter with the risen Jesus. And they suffered excruciating deaths rather than deny it. Every one of their martyrdoms was a deathbed confession, which I tend to believe. Most important, the arch-persecutor Saul, who probably never knew the real Jesus, testified to an overwhelming encounter with the

Jesus whose followers he was executing. That encounter worked a total turnabout in his soul, and he went from arch-persecutor to arch-proselytizer. And he sealed his conviction with martyrdom.

After all those years of unquestioning belief—and then all those years of skepticism—I finally did truly *believe* that Jesus rose from the dead!

Then how could I go back to pretending I was waiting for a Baby Jesus who had already come, and left, and came back again—definitively and forever? How could I manufacture a sad sense of loss on Good Friday when I knew the end of the story was an incandescent triumph?

When I encounter questions like that, I usually set myself to write a book. In trying to formulate an answer for someone else, I find a better, less confused answer for myself. I know that prayer—the *realest* prayer—when we are utterly open and malleable, is like the moments before we go to sleep, when we are finally willing to yield the world to God, or when we are buzzed on booze and yet alone with God, anchorless without God, drifting between this and that obligation, and more than willing to hand the tiller to Someone Else. But is there a book that helps those of us who are not giants of the spiritual life, with easy access to the anchor?

This is my fumbling attempt to provide that book.

It is an attempt, a few times during the day in Lent (or anytime), to recapture a sense of felt remembrance of the events that led up to our liberation from the fear of death, as the Jewish Passover is a felt remembrance of the liberation from Egypt and slavery. It is an attempt to deflect the critical mind and ignite the believing heart. An attempt not to define but to feel.

What this book offers is an opportunity not for Lenten self-denial but for Lenten self-enrichment. It suggests giving up not some material pleasure but taking time—the busyness, the worries, others' expectations—to tap into the energizing Source of all life, enlivening the bustling inter-changes within the tiniest atom, empowering the Spring slowly to overwhelm the winter with new green, inciting rabbits to cavort and consort, calling human beings to some-thing more than mere survival. Rather than denying the self, it offers a chance to affirm that—no matter our sup-posed weaknesses and shortcomings, no matter what *any-one* else thinks of us—the God who lit the farthest star has chosen each of *us*.

The scripture passages in these pages have no official sanction (in either sense, I hope). They are similar to what films mean when they tag "as suggested by" to a title, or like the sketches a neophyte artist might make, in a slightly different idiom, of a masterpiece.

Ash Wednesday

Presence
Great Friend,
I'm not yet up to the total make-over.
Help me proceed, as Italians say,
lentamente, slowly.

Grace
Abba, before the busyness begins, remind me I am dust
You brought to life.

Psalm 51
Lord, like lion and lamb, in Your inmost heart
justice and mercy calmly conjoin in peace.
I own my flaws, my imperfections, my forgiven sins
Of all You have created, humans only
Are from the womb imperfect, capricious, bent—
leaning always toward the easier, lesser.
Perhaps Your reason in making us imperfect
is You so much love growth, evolution, change?
I offer You a willing, unassuming soul.
Surely You will not reject a humble and repentant heart.

Hymn
To ev'rything (turn, turn, turn)
there is a season (turn, turn, turn)
and a time for ev'ry purpose under Heaven.

A time to be born, a time to die;
a time to plant, a time to reap;
a time to kill, a time to laugh,
a time to weep.

To ev'rything (turn, turn, turn)
there is a season (turn, turn, turn)
and a time for ev'ry purpose under Heaven.

A time to build up, a time to break down;
a time to dance, a time to mourn;
a time to cast away stones; a time to gather stones
        together.

To ev'rything (turn, turn, turn)
there is a season (turn, turn, turn)
and a time for ev'ry purpose under Heaven.

A time of love, a time of hate;
a time of war, a time of peace;
a time you may embrace; a time to refrain from
        embracing.

To ev'rything (turn, turn, turn)
there is a season (turn, turn, turn)
and a time for ev'ry purpose under Heaven.

A time to gain, a time to lose;
a time to rend, a time to sew;
a time to love, a time to hate;
A time for peace, I swear it's not too late.

—WORDS FROM THE BOOK OF ECCLESIASTES.
ADAPTATION AND MUSIC BY PETE SEEGER.

Dedication
God, my Friend,
I offer You each moment of this day:
whatever comes—the unexpected challenges,
    diversions from my plans,
        the need-filled glance,
        the expectations and complaints,

the being taken for granted,
the slights and sleights-of-hand.
I'd be grateful if You could keep me aware of my pesky
habits, like . . .
And, between us, perhaps we can enliven the spirits of
those I live and work with, like . . .
Whatever else befalls,
I trust we can cope with it,
together.
Amen.

✛ Daytime

Presence
Great Friend,
the burden is far lighter
knowing Your strong shoulder
is on the other side.

Grace
Abba, help me be honest with myself, about what I *can* do.

Psalm
Because our adoptive Brother is the Prince,
we are now Peers of His Realm, His emissaries,
sent where they would fear to welcome Him.
His awesome goodness, purified in the blood
He now shares with us, negates our flaws and fears.
And the message we are sent to share is this:
"Now is the time. Now is the day you are saved."
—2 CORINTHIANS 5:20–6:2

Hymn
Then God sat down—
On the side of a hill where he could think;
By a deep, wide river he sat down;

With his head in his hands,
God thought and thought,
Till he thought: I'll make me a man!

Up from the bed of the river
God scooped the clay;
And by the bank of the river
He kneeled him down;
And there the great God Almighty
Who lit the sun and fixed it in the sky,
Who flung the stars to the most far corner of the night,
Who rounded the earth in the middle of his hand;
This great God,
Like a mammy bending over her baby,
Kneeled down in the dust
Toiling over a lump of clay
Till he shaped it in is his own image;

Then into it he blew the breath of life,
And man became a living soul.
Amen. Amen.
—JAMES WELDON JOHNSON, "THE CREATION"

Reading

When the job is a labor of love, the sacrifices will present
themselves to the worker—strange as it may seem—in the
guise of enjoyment. . . . The Puritan assumption that all
action disagreeable to the doer is *ipso facto* more meritori-
ous than enjoyable action, is firmly rooted in this exagger-
ated valuation set on pride. . . . The Puritan . . . is inclined
to say, "Of course, So-and-so works very hard and has given
up a good deal for such-and-such cause, but there's no merit
in that—he enjoys it." The merit, of course, lies precisely
in the enjoyment, and the nobility of So-and-so consists in
the very fact that he is the kind of person to whom the
doing of that piece of work is delightful.
—DOROTHY L. SAYERS, *THE MIND OF THE MAKER*

Scripture

Jesus told his friends, "Let your kindness be so unobtrusive even your own left hand can't quite be sure what your right is palming off. If it is a gift, let it go with your full heart, not worrying how worthily it is spent. Trumpeted kindness deludes no one but oneself. Surely not God. When you pray, find a place apart to be with Abba alone, without approving witnesses to say, 'How holy!' And when you do penance, let your manifest joy deceive them all!"

—MATTHEW 6:1–6, 16–18

Closing

God, my Friend, Your mark is on me.
Far more deeply ingrained than Cain's.
Your name is branded into my soul.
The breath of Your life is in me.
Amen.

✟ Evening

Presence

Great Friend,
the end of an imperfect day,
made less so by Your presence in it.
Thank You for carrying it with me.

Grace

Abba, let me forgive myself as lightheartedly as You do.

Psalm

Then Job said to God, "I am overwhelmed!
Now I see—no, truly *feel*—who You are!
Nothing and no one can challenge Your plans.
You asked, 'Who is this man I gave his mind
who dares question my choices from a scope so small?
Do I need my servant's approval before I move?'

I confess it: I babbled of things beyond my bumbling.
You dared me face You down as if Your equal,
Which I am not, and never was, nor will be.
All I knew of You before was husks of hearsay,
fifth-hand rumors, others' empty certitudes.
But now, in my nakedness, I have encountered You—
          YOU!
Now, I loathe my arrogant pretentiousness,
and I humbly repent in dust and ashes."

—Job 42:1–6

Hymn

          WHEN God at first made man,
Having a glasse of blessings standing by;
Let us (said he) poure on him all we can:
Let the world's riches, which dispersed lie,
          Contract into a span.

          So strength first made a way;
Then beautie flow'd, then wisdome, honour, pleasure:
When almost all was out, God made a stay,
Perceiving that alone, of all his treasure,
          Rest in the bottome lay.

          For if I should (said he)
Bestow this jewell also on my creature,
He would adore my gifts in stead of me,
And rest in Nature, not the God of Nature:
          So both should losers be.

          Yet let him keep the rest,
But keep them with repining restlesnesse:
Let him be rich and wearie, that at least,
If goodnesse leade him not, yet wearinesse
          May tosse him to my breast.

—George Herbert, "The Pulley"

Closing
Holy Friend,
unlike Yourself, as You know,
my day is finite,
    slowed down by gravity and time.
While I let go the reins awhile,
I trust they are in better hands than mine.
Amen.

Thursday

✛ Morning

Presence
Great Friend,
I have confidence in myself today
because I trust with all my heart
that You have confidence in me.

Grace
Abba, don't let my self-doubts get in Your way.

Psalm 55
At times, Lord, I'm weary before I even begin.
I have no great enemies like the ones who wrote Your
      psalms,
or at least I lack their heroic sense of drama:
terror, betrayal, cataclysms at every turn.
But I do live in a most bewildering world
where the need for dominance tramples every other,
in the marketplace, the board rooms, the halls of justice
      and law,
more unyielding than cries of the poor, the children, the
      lost.
I beg You for light to see and air to breathe
in a world suffused by shadows, shiftiness, and guile,
where innocence is naivete and trust is for fools.
Fasten my grasp on truth, and stiffen my resolve.
If You haven't given up on us, then neither shall I.

Hymn
What good am I if I'm like all the rest,
If I just turned away, when I see how you're dressed,

If I shut myself off so I can't hear you cry,
What good am I?

What good am I if I know and don't do,
If I see and don't say, if I look right through you,
If I turn a deaf ear to the thunderin' sky,
What good am I?

What good am I while you softly weep
And I hear in my head what you say in your sleep,
And I freeze in the moment like the rest who don't try,
What good am I?

What good am I then to others and me
If I've had every chance and yet still fail to see
If my hands are tied must I not wonder within
Who tied them and why and where must I have been?

What good am I if I say foolish things
And I laugh in the face of what sorrow brings
And I just turn my back while you silently die,
What good am I?
—Bob Dylan, "What Good Am I?"

Dedication
God, my Friend,
I offer You each moment of this day:
whatever comes—the unexpected challenges,
    diversions from my plans,
    the need-filled glance,
    the expectations and complaints,
    the being taken for granted,
    the slights and sleights-of-hand.
I'd be grateful if You could keep me aware of my pesky
    habits, like . . .
And, between us, perhaps we can enliven the spirits of
    those I live and work with, like . . .

Whatever else befalls,
  I trust we can cope with it,
  together.
Amen.

✠ Daytime

Presence
Great Friend,
You made humans alone to learn and love,
  to use our wits to discern what can be changed,
  to open our hearts to those we find repellent.
Ignite my mind and heart with Your life-giving Spirit.

Grace
Abba, to be useful, I must be used.

Psalm 1
How blessed are those who can sense a clever ruse,
who can smell the insolence in those who sneer at truth,
who have no need of You, who can go it all alone!
Yours have found Your will in the ways all things are
            made
and use them as any fool could see You wish.
They are trees rooted by the living waters of Your grace,
whose yield is bountiful and whose shade embraces all.
Not so the self-sufficient, the scornful, the boastful,
colorful as disconnected leaves drifting aimlessly,
worth nothing in the end but being turned to smoke.

Hymn
Make me a channel of your peace:
Where there is hatred, let me bring your love;
Where there is injury, your healing pow'r,
And where there's doubt, true faith in you.

Make me a channel of your peace:
Where there's despair in life let me bring hope;
Where there is darkness—only light,
And where there's sadness, ever joy.

O Spirit, grant that I may never seek
So much to be consoled as to console,
To be understood as to understand,
To be loved as to love with all my soul—

Make me a channel of your peace.
It is in pardoning that we are pardoned,
In giving to all that we receive,
And in dying that we're born to eternal life.

Reading
I was distressed you wouldn't come and have been worrying about what could be the matter. I started to call you up and try to persuade you to change your mind and then I decided I had better mind my own business and didn't do it. Now I am sorry I didn't because I think too many people and especially me mind their own business when their real business is somebody else's business.
—FLANNERY O'CONNOR, *THE HABIT OF BEING*

Scripture
Jesus told them, "The Son of Man has a heavy ordeal ahead. I'm going to be rejected by the religious hierarchy, their teachers, their learned men. I'm going to be executed. Yes. But on the third day I will be back alive again. And you can expect no less yourselves. If any of you wants to be a part of me, you have to put aside your other priorities and imitate mine. Don't run from suffering, embrace it, shoulder your cross—every single day—whatever form it takes. I'm here to show you how to deal with it, with dignity, to discover your true self. If you try to horde your self in security, you

will end up valueless. How could you find the fulfillment
you were born for, if you achieve absolutely everything the
world tells you will make you fulfilled, and yet there's no
true self within you?"

—LUKE 9:22–25

Closing
God, my Friend, I'm too tactful, too reserved.
    How can I embrace the burden of a cross,
    if I'm too reticent to say,
    "Forgive me, but can I help?"
Amen.

✛ Evening

Presence
Great Friend,
the day winds down, and so do I,
    like a clock in need of winding.
Silently, in the night, ready me
    to dis-purse my time for you
    tomorrow.

Grace
Abba, thank You for the chance to be useful today.

Psalm 51
Open-handed Lord of love, hear me.
Help me to accept that my sins are cleansed,
and I, unworthy, am washed as white as snow.
Fill the emptiness my sins have left behind.
Create in me a heart as responsive as a child's.
You don't want sacrifices, or I would offer them.
You don't want me to give up things but take things on.
My offering is a humble spirit and a ready heart.

Hymn

Slowly the evening changes into the clothes
held for it by a row of ancient trees; you look: and two
      worlds grow separate from you,
one ascending to heaven, another, that falls;

and leave you, belonging not wholly to either one,
not quite as dark as the house that remains silent,
not quite as certainly sworn to eternity
as that which becomes a star each night and rises—

and leave you (unsayably to disentangle) your life
with all its immensity and fear and great ripening,
so that, all but bounded, all but understood,
it is by turns stone in you and star.
     —RAINER MARIA RILKE, TRANSLATED BY CLIFF CREGO

Closing

Holy Friend,
I place my day back in Your hands.
Thanks for the gift
   of everything.
Amen.

Friday

✠ Morning

Presence
Great Friend,
today we fast and abstain,
as a trivial reminder
  of how gifted we are.

Grace
Abba, so many worthier didn't wake today. I did.

Psalm 30
Lord, when I feel helpless and inept,
You've taught me to tip-toe boldly over quicksand
that I thought too daunting, impassible, impossible.
Let my family, the saints, shout Your praise in heaven!
At times, the Shadow in me *does* tempt me to gloat.
To brag, "How well I've done! And by myself!"
But when my eyes drift from You to the mirror,
I begin to sink into the quagmire of clumsy me.
Such ploys You have—to remind me I'm not You!
You make mourning into music, and I have the itch to
    dance!
How can I be silent about the gift of life You've given?
Lord, my God, how can I thank You enough?

Hymn
Have Thine own way, Lord,
Have Thine own way;
Thou art the Potter,
I am the clay.
Mold me and make me
After Thy will,

While I am waiting,
Yielded and still.

Have Thine own way, Lord,
Have Thine own way;
Hold o'er my being
Absolute sway.
Fill with Thy Spirit
Till all shall see
Christ only, always,
Living in me.
—ADELAIDE ADDISON POLLARD (1862–1934)

Dedication
God, my Friend,
I offer You each moment of this day:
whatever comes—the unexpected challenges,
   diversions from my plans,
   the need-filled glance,
   the expectations and complaints,
   the being taken for granted,
   the slights and sleights-of-hand.
I'd be grateful if You could keep me aware of my pesky
       habits, like . . .
And, between us, perhaps we can enliven the spirits of
       those I live and work with, like . . .
Whatever else befalls,
   I trust we can cope with it,
   together.
Amen.

✝ Daytime

Presence
Great Friend,
let the Lenten gift I give You not be lean.
Let it be open-handed, sharing, joyful.

Grace
Abba, help me penetrate Your Son's disguises.

Psalm
The Lord says, "Shout as loud as you can shout!
My people claim they accept My ways, study them,
fast because it's something they're told to do.
The truth is, when they fast, they become short-tempered,
focused on the emptiness in their bellies
when their empty souls should be hungry for Me!
Is that the kind of fast they think I want?
Pious, empty faces as a sign of selflessness?
The kind of fast I want is that you share your food
with the hungry, donate clothes you haven't worn in a year,
choose *one* worthy cause and give whatever you can.
Give up every whisper of contempt for the world's losers.
Forgive their foolish choices and lack of foresight.
Then I will bring dawn into the darkness of your souls,
and your day will bring life-giving light."
—Isaiah 58:1–9

Hymn
A fervent prayer rose up to heaven,
A fragile soul was losing ground
Sorting through this earthly babble,
Heaven heard the sound.
It was a life of no distinction,
No successes, only tries.
Yet, gazing down on this unlovely one,
There was love in Heaven's eyes.

In Heaven's Eyes, there are no losers,
In Heaven's Eyes, no hopeless cause.
Only people like you, with feelings like me
And we're amazed at the grace we can find
In Heaven's Eyes.

The orphaned child, the wayward father,
The homeless traveler in the rain
When life goes by and no one bothers,
Heaven feels the pain.
Looking down, God sees each heartache,
Knows each sorrow, hears each cry,
And looking up, we'll see compassion's
Fire ablaze in Heaven's Eyes.

Reading

We can ignore, but we can nowhere evade, the presence of God. The world is crowded with Him. He walks everywhere incognito. And the incognito is not always hard to penetrate. The real labour is to remember, to attend. In fact, to come awake. Still more, to remain awake.

—C. S. Lewis, *Letters to Malcolm*

Scripture

Some of John's followers approached Jesus and asked, "How is it we, and the Pharisees, and true religious people fast dutifully and often, and your people never fast at all?" Jesus chuckled. "Do you expect people to tighten their belts and turn away their faces from a wedding feast when the bridegroom is still with them?" He shook his head, ruefully. "How foolish and quick to judge you are! When the bridegroom is taken away—and he will be—then they can mourn and fast. But the bridegroom is coming back! And then the wedding feast will never end!"

—Matthew 9:14–15

Closing

God, my Friend,
the more of myself I give away,
the more I have to give.
Amen.

✠ Evening

Presence
Great Friend,
while I rest in your shadow,
there are no shadows.

Grace
Abba, into Your hands I commend my spirit.

Psalm 25
Lord, when I'm at Your side, I hold my head up high.
I won't let the wearisome cynics wear me down.
Remember the millennia of Your mercies, Lord,
and forgive my foolishnesses, which have been many.
Correct my misdirections and rejections
of Your invitations to be better than my fears.
Without You at the core of my soul, my life's
No more than mismatched beads without a string.
But with You, I'm all together, whole.
Remind me, when I feel alone, I'm not.

Hymn
Lord, take my hand and lead me
Upon life's way;
Direct, protect, and feed me
From day to day.
Without your grace and favor
I go astray;
So take my hand, O Savior,
And lead the way.

Lord, when the tempest rages,
I need not fear;
For you, the Rock of Ages,
Are always near.

Close by your side abiding,
I fear no foe,
For when your hand is guiding,
In peace I go.

Lord, when the shadows lengthen
And night has come,
I know that you will strengthen
My steps toward home,
And nothing can impede me,
O blessed Friend!
So take my hand and lead me
Unto the end.

Closing
Holy Friend,
take today as my best gift to You.
Once again, imperfect,
but the best I have to give.
Amen.

Saturday

✠ Morning

Presence
Great Friend,
when I pull off the weekday road,
    the quiet is almost palpable.
Infuse this serenity into my heart
    so I can energize myself once again.

Grace
Abba, give me perspective, and her sister, peace.

Psalm 69
Lord, the world I live in has become a swamp.
Voices far more powerful and seductive than mine
make the trivial important and the meaningful trite—
love, loyalty, and death are now just toys and games
played by beautiful children in grown-up bodies
before grimly docile, dourly etherized millions.
How do I coax the grateful dead to life?
To them, what I offer and live is preposterous!
Offering self-forgetfulness to the self-absorbed?
Sacrifice to those who scorn even inconvenience?
Who honor commitments until they begin to cost?
At times, I grow disheartened like Elijah, Jeremiah,
and all idealist fools who get hooted from the orgy.
Stiffen my spine! Fire my heart! Ignite my soul!
My unfailing trust is my offering to You.

Hymn
When, in disgrace with fortune and men's eyes,
I all alone beweep my outcast state

And trouble heaven with my bootless cries
And look upon myself and curse my fate,
Wishing me like to one more rich in hope,
Featured like him, like him with friends possess'd,
Desiring this man's art and that man's scope,
With what I most enjoy contented least;
Yet in these thoughts myself almost despising,
Haply I think on Thee, and then my state,
Like to the lark at break of day arising
From sullen earth, sings hymns at heaven's gate;
For Thy sweet love remember'd such wealth brings
That then I scorn to change my state with kings.
—WILLIAM SHAKESPEARE, SONNET 29

Dedication
God, my Friend,
I offer You each moment of this day:
whatever comes—the unexpected challenges,
    diversions from my plans,
    the need-filled glance,
    the expectations and complaints,
    the being taken for granted,
    the slights and sleights-of-hand.
I'd be grateful if You could keep me aware of my pesky
    habits, like . . .
And, between us, perhaps we can enliven the spirits of
    those I live and work with, like . . .
Whatever else befalls,
    I trust we can cope with it,
    together.
Amen.

✛ Daytime

Presence
Great Friend,

it helps to know
I'm not alone.

Grace
Abba, help me remember the simple taste of bread.

Psalm 86
Lord, I make bold to ask You to hear my prayer.
I depend on You from morning until night.
I serve You and trust You because You are my God.
You made me to be happy, but I'm in need of help
discerning just what happiness truly means.
The things others take for gods are gilded husks,
promising a joy that isn't theirs to give.
Only You can fill my God-sized emptiness.
I reach up my soul for You to gladden it
so I can offer Your amnesty with genuine delight.
With Your gentle, powerful hand, keep me on my feet.

Hymn
Break Thou the Bread of Life,
Dear Lord, to me,
As Thou didst break the loaves
Beside the sea;
Beyond the sacred page
I seek Thee, Lord;
My spirit pants for Thee,
O Living Word.
Bless Thou the truth, dear Lord,
To me, to me,
As Thou didst bless the bread
By Galilee;
Then shall all bondage cease,
All fetters fall,
And I shall find my peace,
My All in all.

—MARY LATHBURY

Reading

Well, toward morning the conversation turned on the Eucharist, which I, being the Catholic, was obviously supposed to defend. Mrs. Broadwater said when she was a child and received the Host, she thought of it as the Holy Ghost, He being the "most portable" person of the Trinity; now she thought of it as a symbol and implied that it was a pretty good one. I then said, in a very shaky voice, "Well, if it's a symbol, to hell with it."

—FLANNERY O'CONNOR, *The Habit of Being*

Scripture

When Jesus got news of John's murder, he slipped away with his friends to a lonely place where they could be by themselves. But news got round, and people began to come from all over, and they were waiting for them when they beached. So Jesus felt profound pity for them and healed their sick. But when evening came, the disciples came to him and said, "Have you noticed the time? Send these people off, and maybe they can buy food in some village nearby." Jesus smiled. "No need for that. We'll feed them." They knitted their brows. "We have only five loaves and two fish for ourselves." So Jesus said, "Bring them to me. Have the people sit on the grass." He took the five loaves and two fish and said a blessing. Then he slowly began breaking them up and giving them to the disciples to pass around. All the people there ate their fill, and the leftover scraps filled twelve baskets. There were five thousand men in that crowd, not to mention the women and children.

—MATTHEW 14:13–21

Closing

God, my Friend,
help me
to break myself up, too,
and hand round the pieces.
Amen.

✢ Evening

Presence
Great Friend,
honest humility has to admit
we did an all-right job today.

Grace
Abba, teach me that honest pride is not arrogance.

Psalm
"Come to Me, you who toil and are burdened.
I will be your refuge and your rest.
I share your yoke with you, and I understand.
Don't be afraid. I'm gentle and humble-hearted.
I offer you easement and a purpose for your labor.
If we share it, the yoke is easy, the burden light."
—MATTHEW 11:28–30

Hymn
Jesus! I am resting, resting
In the joy of what Thou art;
I am finding out the greatness
Of Thy loving heart.
Thou hast bid me gaze upon Thee,
And Thy beauty fills my soul,
For, by Thy transforming power,
Thou hast made me whole.

—J. S. PIGOTT

Closing
Holy Friend,
thank You once again
    for the chance to serve.
Amen.

First Sunday

✠ Morning

Presence
Great Friend,
in these days, the Church forbids "Alleluias."
But when I know what I believe,
they're difficult to hold back.

Grace
Abba, *lentamente, lentamente.*

Psalm
When Noah and his family disembarked,
God summoned them together and he said,
"I now make unending Covenant with you
and with everyone born from this day on,
and with all living beings you've saved from death.
We're starting all over again, you and I.
You've come through the waters of death, brand new!
Never again will the seas destroy all I have made.
As a sign of this new union of heaven and earth,
I will set a rainbow binding the two in peace—
every shade and tint blended in one arc,
prismed from the white-hot light of My love,
as those of every human color are now My people.
My bow in the clouds is a sign of My love-pact with you,
My promise forever to make all things new again."
                                        —Genesis 9:8–15

Hymn
My heart leaps up when I behold
    A rainbow in the sky.

So was it when my life began,
So is it now I am a man,
So be it when I shall grow old
    Or let me die!

The child is father of the man:
And I could wish my days to be
Bound each to each by natural piety.
                    —WILLIAM WORDSWORTH

Dedication
God, my Friend,
I offer You each moment of this day:
whatever comes—the unexpected challenges,
    diversions from my plans,
    the need-filled glance,
    the expectations and complaints,
    the being taken for granted,
    the slights and sleights-of-hand.
I'd be grateful if You could keep me aware of my pesky
        habits, like . . .
And, between us, perhaps we can enliven the spirits of
        those I live and work with, like . . .
Whatever else befalls,
    I trust we can cope with it,
        together.
Amen.

✛ Daytime

Presence
Great Friend,
we gather today at Your table
to celebrate our freedom
    from the fear of guilt,
    from the fear of death,
    from the fear of ultimate meaninglessness.

Grace
Abba, make me feel renewed again.

Psalm
Beloved: Christ did it for us, once for all,
carried our sins in his flesh through the waters of death,
the never-contaminated died for the so-often defiled.
He irradiated the cesspool as clean as a mountain lake
and offered its purifying waters whenever we choose,
brought life even to the depths, to the realms of the dead.
In the time of Noah, only eight were saved,
but now God's arms open to welcome all and any—
"Come one! Come all! Whenever you are ready!"
This is no bodily bath but a renewal of the soul
that scours the conscience clean as a just-born child's.
That freedom is guaranteed by our brother's rebirth,
a gift he gives prodigally to all who feel the need.
—1 Peter 3:18–22

Hymn
I will sing the wondrous story
Of the Christ who died for me.
How He left His home in glory
For the cross of Calvary.
I was lost, but Jesus found me,
Found the sheep that went astray,
Threw His loving arms around me,
Drew me back into His way.

I was bruised, but Jesus healed me;
Faint was I from many a fall;
Sight was gone, and fears possessed me,
But He freed me from them all.
Days of darkness still come o'er me,
Sorrow's paths I often tread,
But the Savior still is with me;
By His hand I'm safely led.

He will keep me till the river
Rolls its waters at my feet;
Then He'll bear me safely over,
Where the loved ones I shall meet.
Yes, I'll sing the wondrous story
Of the Christ who died for me,
Sing it with the saints in glory,
Gathered by the crystal sea.

—Francis H. Rowley

Reading

The Godly Goodness that has banished every envy from its own Self, burns in Itself; and sparkling so, It shows eternal beauties. All that derives directly from this Goodness is everlasting, since the seal of Goodness impresses an imprint that never alters. Whatever rains from It immediately is fully free, for it is not constrained by an influence of other things. Even as it conforms to that Goodness, so does it please It more; the Sacred Ardor that gleams in all things is most bright within those things most like Itself.

—Dante Alighieri, Paradiso,
translated by Allen Mandelbaum

Scripture

When Jesus stumbled up the banks of Jordan where John had baptized him, the terrifying voice still thundering in his soul, "You are my Son! You are the One!" the Spirit hurled him into the wilderness for forty days and nights, to have this vocation tested. "Ha, ha! If you are the Son of God, turn these stones into bread, and they'll flock to you like sheep. No one can resist bread! Fling yourself from the Temple top. They can't resist a miracle. That's all they want from you! Take on the power of Caesar, and coerce them to goodness!" And when Evil left him, rejected, angels ministered to him. When John was arrested, Jesus came forth up north in Galilee, proclaiming the New Covenant: "The time of fulfillment is now! The new Kingdom of God

is at your fingertips! Change your lives—your whole way
of looking at what's important. I've brought good news!"
—MARK 1:12–15 (WITH MATTHEW 3)

Closing
God, my Friend,
I'm told
> You rested from your labors on the first Sabbath day,
> and Your Son scandalized small-minded folk by
> > enjoying food and a drink too zestfully.
I need not apologize, then,
> for following your examples.
Amen.

✛ Evening

Presence
Great Friend,
the bridge over the abyss
> between rational proofs
> and sureness of You,
is a rainbow.

Grace
Abba, point the way, and I'll follow, wherever.

Psalm
Just as they'd come to the verge of the Red Sea,
the Hebrews saw a pillar of dust behind them,
and they shouted in terror, "Were there no graves in
> Egypt
that you led us to die in this nowhere place?"
But the Lord whispered to Moses, "Lift your staff!"
As he did, a whirlwind careened toward them from the
> east.
The waters flew up into huge palisades,

and a canyon of dry land opened between the waves.
Thousands of the people followed the Lord through the
        sea
into the moonscape desert toward the Promised Land.
                 —Exodus 14:10–22

Hymn

I cried a tear
You wiped it dry
I was confused
You cleared my mind
I sold my soul
You bought it back for me
And held me up and gave me dignity
Somehow you needed me.

You gave me strength
To stand alone again
To face the world
Out on my own again
You put me high upon a pedestal
So high that I could almost see eternity
You needed me
You needed me.

And I can't believe it's you I can't believe it's true
I needed you and you were there
And I'll never leave, why should I leave
I'd be a fool
'Cause I've finally found someone who really cares.

You held my hand
When it was cold
When I was lost
You took me home
You gave me hope

When I was at the end
And turned my lies
Back into truth again
You even called me friend.

You gave me strength
To stand alone again
To face the world
Out on my own again
You put me high upon a pedestal
So high that I could almost see eternity
You needed me
You needed me.

—RANDY GOODRUM

Closing
Holy Friend,
the Sabbath ends.
A new week of opportunities awaits.
Help me improvise well.
Amen.

First Monday

♦ Morning

Presence
Great Friend,
let this be not just "another week."
Let's make it *shine*!

Grace
Abba, help me be ready when You sneak up on me.

Psalm 123
I lift my eyes, Lord, though You are everywhere.
Just as a servant is alert to his master's desires,
and a maid anticipates her mistress's wish,
make me sensitive to the flickers of need in others' faces.
Prepare me, when I offer help, for embarrassed refusal,
or shy withdrawal, or misunderstanding, or outright
        scorn.
Help me accept the painful truth that
Some are not ready for freedom or love or joy.

Hymn
Morning has broken like the first morning.
Blackbird has spoken like the first bird.
Praise for the singing, praise for the morning,
Praise for them springing fresh from the Word.

Sweet the rain's new fall, sunlit from heaven,
Like the first dew fall on the first grass.
Praise for the sweetness of the wet garden,
Sprung in completeness where His feet pass.

Mine is the sunlight, mine is the morning,
Born of the One Light Eden saw play.
Praise with elation, praise every morning,
God's recreation of the new day.

—ELEANOR FARJEON

Dedication
God, my Friend,
I offer You each moment of this day:
whatever comes—the unexpected challenges,
   diversions from my plans,
   the need-filled glance,
   the expectations and complaints,
   the being taken for granted,
   the slights and sleights-of-hand.
I'd be grateful if You could keep me aware of my pesky
     habits, like . . .
And, between us, perhaps we can enliven the spirits of
     those I live and work with, like . . .
Whatever else befalls,
   I trust we can cope with it,
    together.
Amen.

✝ Daytime

Presence
Great Friend,
my family is no longer my only kin,
every man, woman, and child is part of what I am,
in every place on the face of the earth,
unto the heights of heaven.

Grace
Abba, make me great-hearted, as You are.

Psalm

The Lord said to Moses, "Be holy—whole—as I am.
Respect those who gave you life, and honor the Sabbath.
Do not cheat, steal, lie, make promises you won't keep.
That brings disgrace on Me, the Lord your God.
Don't take advantage of others' weakness or deceive
      them.
Don't hold back just wages, even overnight.
Have patience with the mute. Don't tease the blind.
Be honest and fair, with no partiality—to rich or poor.
Don't erode reputations with idle gossip and rumors.
When your neighbor's life is in peril, don't just stand by.
Don't cherish grudges; have the courage to set things
      right.
Be as sensitive to your neighbor as you are for yourself.
I am GOD!"

—LEVITICUS 19:1–2, 11–18

Hymn

Blest be the tie that binds
Our hearts in Christian love;
The fellowship of kindred minds
Is like to that above.

Before our Father's throne
We pour our ardent pray'rs;
Our fears, our hopes, our aims are one,
Our comforts and our cares.

We share our mutual woes,
Our mutual burdens bear;
And often for each other flows
The sympathizing tear.

From sorrow, toil, and pain,
And sin we shall be free:

And perfect love and friendship reign
Through all eternity.

—JOHN FAWCETT (1782)

Reading

But if God love me, Celie, I don't have to do all that. Unless I want to. There's a lot of other things I can do that I speck God likes.

Like what? I ast.

Oh, she say. I can lay back and just admire stuff. Be happy. Have a good time.

Well, this sound like blasphemy sure nuff.

She say, Celie, tell the truth, have you ever found God in church? I never did. I just found a bunch of folks hoping for him to show. Any God I ever felt in church I brought in with me. And I think all the other folks did too. They come to church to *share* God, not to *find* God.

—ALICE WALKER, *THE COLOR PURPLE*

Scripture

Jesus said, "When the Son of Man comes, blazing with glory, to ratify the decisions each one has made in life, his gaze alone will send all before him milling into two different groups, without knowing why, but like sheep with sheep on his right and goats with goats on His left. Then he will say to those on his right, 'Come, because you radiate my Father's love. His Kingdom belongs to you. When I was hungry, you made sure I had a meal. When I was thirsty for some kind of recognition, you saw me and reached out. I was alone and rejected, and you welcomed me, naked and you shared your clothes with me, sick and you visited me, in prison and wrote me again and again.' The ones who had lived as my Father hoped, will be puzzled. 'You?' they will ask. 'Lord, when did we ever see *you* hungry or thirsty, alone, naked, imprisoned—and reach out to you? If we'd known, of course we would have, but. . . . ' And the King will smile at them. 'Whenever you did any of those things to my least appealing sisters and brothers, you did it to me.' And to the others he will say, 'Whenever you passed by an empty hand, whenever you scorned the unattractive and "different," whenever you ignored those sick with grief or confusion or locked off in defensive anonymity, you degraded me. Go away. I've forgotten your names.'"

—MATTHEW 25:31–46

Closing
God, my Friend,
You calmed the Chaos in the beginning.
Your Son calmed the troubled waters.
Teach me to calm troubled hearts.
Amen.

✟ Evening

Presence
Great Friend,
everything makes so much more sense
when I yield dominance to You.

Grace
Abba, I offer You my wilfulness. Take hold of it for me.

Psalm 19
How clearly the night sky reveals Your splendor!
Uncounted fire-folk blazing Your endless glory.
Each body moving with stately pace in grand carouse,
yet each unique as every six-spoked snowflake,
but still moving predictably, submissive to Your will.
If only my will were biddable as measureless galaxies,
or simple stones, or daisies or dutiful spiders
that follow Your laws with no doubt or hesitation.
Of all your creatures, you let me ponder and choose
to offer my grateful love in chosen servitude.

Hymn
Elder Father, though thine eyes
Shine with hoary mysteries,
Canst thou tell what in the heart
Of a cowslip blossom lies?

Smaller than all lives that be,
Secret as the deepest sea,
Stands a little house of seeds,
Like an elfin's granary.

Speller of the stones and weeds,
Skilled in Nature's crafts and creeds,
Tell me what is in the heart
Of the smallest of the seeds:

God Almighty, and with Him
Cherubim and Seraphim,
Filling all eternity—
Adonai Elohim.

—G. K. CHESTERTON

Closing
Holy Friend,
I gratefully accept
Your gift of peace.
Amen.

First Tuesday

✠ Morning

Presence
Great Friend,
let my work today,
    especially the tedious times,
be a prayer I offer You.

Grace
Abba, open all I am and fill it.

Psalm
Turn to the Lord, and pray to Him. He is very near.
Let the downcast leave their obsessions behind
and turn their thoughts from themselves to the Lord.
His mercy comes more swiftly than lightning
and gentler than snow. "My thoughts," says the Lord,
"are not as narrow and pinched and picky as yours,
and what I value is as distant from what you crave
as you yourself are from the farmost star.
My word is like life-giving rain for parched souls.
Open your soul so that I may make it live again."
                                    —Isaiah 55:6–10

Hymn
Praise the Lord, rise up rejoicing,
Worship, thanks, devotion voicing:
Glory be to God on high!
Christ, your cross and passion sharing,
By this Eucharist declaring
Yours the final victory.

Scattered flock, one shepherd sharing,
Lost and lonely, one voice hearing,
Ears attentive to the word;
By the blood new life receiving,
In the body, firm believing,
We are yours, and you the Lord.

Sins forgiven, wrongs forgiving,
We go forth alert and living
In your Spirit, strong and free.
Partners in your new creation,
Seeking peace in ev'ry nation,
May we faithful foll'wers be.

—H. C. A. GAUNT

Dedication

God, my Friend,
I offer You each moment of this day:
whatever comes—the unexpected challenges,
    diversions from my plans,
    the need-filled glance,
    the expectations and complaints,
    the being taken for granted,
    the slights and sleights-of-hand.
I'd be grateful if You could keep me aware of my pesky
        habits, like . . .
And, between us, perhaps we can enliven the spirits of
        those I live and work with, like . . .
Whatever else befalls,
    I trust we can cope with it,
    together.
Amen.

✚ Daytime

Presence
Great Friend,
I yield center stage
to One who knows how to handle it.

Grace
Abba, thank You for allowing me a role.

Psalm 34
My prayer of praise to You swells my heart!
You came further than I to calm my anxious fears.
Your strong arm braces the backs of the weary,
the oppressed, the helpless, the troubled, the lost.
Even lions go hungry, but the faithful have all they need.
You're there when I say, "I *can't!* But if You ask, I'll try."
Does anyone want to be happy? Then speak only truth,
guard your neighbor's weakness, bear troubles bravely.
The Lord is alert and ready as a newborn's mother
for the cries of those in need who trust His loving.
He can't bear your burden for you, but He can carry you.

Hymn
What a friend we have in Jesus,
All our sins and griefs to bear!
What a privilege to carry
Ev'rything to God in prayer!
Oh, what peace we often forfeit,
Oh, what needless pain we bear,
All because we do not carry
Ev'rything to God in prayer!

Have we trials and temptations?
Is there trouble anywhere?
We should never be discouraged,

Take it to the Lord in prayer:
Can we find a friend so faithful
Who will all our sorrows share?
Jesus knows our ev'ry weakness,
Take it to the Lord in prayer.

—JOSEPH M. SCRIVEN (1857)

Reading

To pray successfully without words one needs to be "at the top of one's form." Otherwise the mental acts become merely imaginative or emotional acts—and a fabricated emotion is a miserable affair. When the gold moments come, when God enables one really to pray without words, who but a fool would reject the gift? But He does not give it—anyway not to me—day in, day out. My mistake was what Pascal, if I remember rightly, calls "Error of Stoicism": thinking we can do always what we can do sometimes.

—C. S. LEWIS, *LETTERS TO MALCOLM*

Scripture

Jesus said, "When you pray, don't rattle off a lot of words, explaining things your Father already knows. Don't bargain, or bribe, or offer your good deeds as collateral, as if He were your banker. Open yourself, and rest in him, to know you are never alone. If you need words, pray simply: 'Our Abba, in heaven and here and everywhere we turn, may Your hallowed name be honored. Help us be your agents in setting the world more right, with the love and forgiveness that govern the Kingdom in heaven. Grant us today the food we need. Forgive us our transgressions against your love, just as we forgive those who offend us. Don't allow us to be tempted beyond our strength, and keep us untainted by Evil.' If you forgive those who wrong you, your Father in heaven will forgive you. But if you fail to forgive, how can you expect to be forgiven?"

—MATTHEW 6:7–15

Closing

God, my Friend,
take my most precious grudges and complaints,
　　my resentments and resistance to forgiving,
and pulverize them in Your powerful hands.
Amen.

✢ Evening

Presence

Great Friend,
I return the part of this world you entrusted to me.
I believe I tried my honest best
　　to make it better.

Grace

Abba, let us share just a moment of peace.

Psalm

We who feel strong in the faith should not belittle
those who seem weaker and less committed than we.
Instead, we should bolster them with our kindness and
　　　　care.
Don't make your offer "Be like me" but "Can I help?"
The Christ we serve didn't come to please himself,
but as scripture says, "I bear every insult hurled at you."
The word of God is a summons to hope and patience,
and may He, the source of all forbearance and faith,
encourage you to be as dependable and steady as He.
so that all of you, with one voice, may praise
the one Father we share with each other and with Christ.
　　　　　　　　　　　　　　　—Romans 15:1–6

Hymn

Soft as the voice of an Angel,
Breathing a lesson unheard,

Hope with a gentle persuasion
Whispers her comforting word.
Wait, till the darkness is over,
Wait, till the tempest is done,
Hope for the sunshine tomorrow
After the shower is gone.

Whispering—whispering—hope,
Oh, how welcome thy voice,
Oh, how welcome thy voice!
Making my . . . making my heart
In its sorrow rejoice.

If in the dusk of the twilight,
Dim be the region afar,
Will not the deepening darkness
Brighten the glimmering star?
Then, when the night is upon us,
Why should the heart sink away?
When the dark midnight is over
Watch for the breaking of day.

—ALICE HAWTHORNE

Closing
Holy Friend,
I wrap up this day,
    somewhat clumsily, like a child's gift,
    inexpert, perhaps, but heartfelt.
Amen.

First Wednesday

✤ Morning

Presence
Great Friend,
no matter how canny or cunning we become,
sooner or later, Your will *will* be done.

Grace
Abba, help me be sensitive to Your hints.

Psalm
After trying, in stubborn conviction of his unworthiness,
to run a world away from God's wishes for him,
Jonah finally obeyed and grumped five hundred miles
to pagan Nineveh, so large it took three days to cross.
Convinced he was a fool, he began to shout God's
      message:
"Repent! Or in forty days you'll be blasted t'hell!"
People stopped in their tracks—vendors, whores,
      officials—
no one of whom had a conscience without its burdens.
When the Ninevite king, with a heavier conscience than
      most,
heard the message, unsure if this alien was just a lunatic
or the legitimate legate of some all-powerful god,
he proclaimed that all should fast in sackcloth and reform
their wicked lives. And all the Ninevites obeyed.
God saw their heartfelt attempts to change their ways
and reciprocated by changing His mind, too.
           —JONAH 3:1–10

Hymn

If there is to be peace in the world
There must be peace in the nations

If there is to be peace in the nations
There must be peace in the cities

If there is to be peace in the cities
There must be peace between neighbours

If there is to be peace between neighbours
There must be peace in the home

If there is to be peace in the home
There must be peace in the heart

—LAO-TSE

Dedication

God, my Friend,
I offer You each moment of this day:
whatever comes—the unexpected challenges,
   diversions from my plans,
   the need-filled glance,
   the expectations and complaints,
   the being taken for granted,
   the slights and sleights-of-hand.
I'd be grateful if You could keep me aware of my pesky
     habits, like . . .
And, between us, perhaps we can enliven the spirits of
     those I live and work with, like . . .
Whatever else befalls,
   I trust we can cope with it,
   together.
Amen.

✢ Daytime

Presence
Great Friend,
if there is anything in my ways
   in need of change,
find some way to let me know.

Grace
Abba, let me be unafraid to think with my heart as well.

Psalm
"It's *never* too late for you to come back," says the
       Lord,
"Change your indolent habits, not just your clothes."
Since time began, the Lord's become quite practiced
in patience, forbearance, tolerance, leniency.
He's changed His mind before—Adam and Eve,
who betrayed Him first, Noah and his eccentric brood,
coward Gideon, trickster Jonah, weasel Moses.
How many times has He embraced Israel, the whore?
The world itself is teaching you. Just look!
Buds along the branches, flowers gulping sun.
The Lord's eternal urge to start over again!
"I will ceaselessly rain down my life-giving Spirit,"
says the Lord. "Your sons and daughters will dream
       dreams,
a new life you never dared imagine! Cherish them."
                —JOEL 2:12–14, 21–24, 28–29

Hymn
I live my life in growing rings
which move out over the things around me.
Perhaps I'll never complete the last,
but that's what I mean to try.

I'm circling around God, around the ancient tower,
and I've been circling thousands of years;
and I still don't know: am I a falcon, a storm
or a great song.
—Rainer Maria Rilke, translated by Cliff Crego

Reading

[Jesus] preaches but He does not lecture. He uses paradox, proverb, exaggeration, parable, irony; even (I mean no irreverence) the "wisecrack." He utters maxims which, like popular proverbs, if rigorously taken, may seem to contradict one another. His teaching therefore cannot be grasped by the intellect alone, cannot be "got up," as if it were a "subject." If we try to do that with it, we shall find Him the most elusive of teachers. He hardly ever gave a straight answer to a straight question. He will not be, in the way we want, "pinned down." The attempt is (again, I mean no irreverence) like trying to bottle a sunbeam.

—C. S. Lewis, *Reflections on the Psalms*

Scripture

As the people gathered round him, Jesus said, "How wrong-headed this world has become! They want miracles, shows of power, sensations. But the only miracle they're going to witness is the miraculous change of heart that Jonah brought about. Just as Jonah shook up the smug and complacent in pagan Nineveh, the Son of Man was sent to work the same turnabout. On the Judgment Day, the pagan Queen of Sheba will stand up and accuse the closed-minded of today, because she journeyed endless miles just to hear Solomon's wisdom. And I tell you truly, there is a greater than Solomon here. On the Judgment Day, the pagan Ninevites will stand and point the finger at you, because they repented when Jonah preached. And I tell you truly, there is a greater than Jonah here!"

—Luke 11:29–32

Closing

God, my Friend,
I accept that You gave me a mind
   not to come to comforting certitudes
   but to enjoy Your puzzling me.
Amen.

✠ Evening

Presence

Great Friend,
it's so good to pull out of the race
   and catch my breath,
   and see the world as it truly is.

Grace

Abba, give me the heart of a child but not a child's mind.

Psalm 5

Lord, strengthen my mind against the sly seductions,
the siren songs that confront me wherever I turn,
that alchemize leaden things to gold:
the voices that glorify greed and surfaces,
that make me crave what no one truly needs,
that entice me to focus all values on myself.
Their words are sinuous, cunning, and deceitful as
        snakes.
Let me not be one of the suckers born every minute.
Remind me the Grail they offer is lead and empty.
Teach me to laugh at their shallow, carnival world.

Hymn

Lord Jesus Christ, with us abide,
For round us falls the eventide;
Nor let Thy Word, that heavenly light,
For us be ever veiled in night.

In these last days of sore distress
Grant us, dear Lord, true steadfastness
That pure we keep, till life is spent,
Thy holy Word and Sacrament.

Lord Jesus, help, Thy Church uphold,
For we are sluggish, thoughtless, cold.
Oh, prosper well Thy Word of grace
And spread its truth in every place!

Oh, grant that in Thy holy Word
We here may live and die, dear Lord;
And when our journey endeth here,
Receive us into glory there.

—NIKOLAUS SELNECKER (1530–92)

Closing
Holy Friend,
with a grateful sigh,
I unstrap the armor
   and give myself up to peace.
Amen.

First Thursday

✤ Morning

Presence
Great Friend,
my body and mind are awake.
Now, quicken my soul!

Grace
Abba, help me comprehend how truly fortunate and gifted
I am.

Psalm 51
Have mercy on me, God of faithful love.
Let Your endless goodness absorb my offenses.
Transform my weaknesses into strength.
I am well aware of them. Perhaps, too aware.
But I want no more than to do what You would have me
            do.
For reasons of Your own, You made us all imperfect,
and by that very gift inviting us to reach
beyond what others are willing to settle for.
The only sacrifice that fulfills Your will
is to purify my heart of all that is not Your will.

Hymn
When I can read my title clear
To mansions in the skies,
I'll bid farewell to ev'ry fear
And wipe my weeping eyes.

And wipe my weeping eyes,
And wipe my weeping eyes,

I'll bid farewell to every fear,
And wipe my weeping eyes.

Should earth against my soul engage,
And fiery darts be hurled,
Then I can smile at Satan's rage
And face a frowning world.

My God, my heav'n, my all,
My God, my heav'n, my all,
May I but safely reach my home,
My God, my heav'n, my all.

Dedication
God, my Friend,
I offer You each moment of this day:
whatever comes—the unexpected challenges,
    diversions from my plans,
    the need-filled glance,
    the expectations and complaints,
    the being taken for granted,
    the slights and sleights-of-hand.
I'd be grateful if You could keep me aware of my pesky
        habits, like . . .
And, between us, perhaps we can enliven the spirits of
        those I live and work with, like . . .
Whatever else befalls,
    I trust we can cope with it,
        together.
Amen.

✦ Daytime

Presence
Great Friend,
let me pray as if everything depended on You,

and work as if everything depended on me,
    and, most important, remember that neither is true.

Grace
Abba, remind me Your viewpoint is incomprehensibly
broader than mine.

Psalm 138
My heart brims over with thanks, O Lord.
It's too much to grasp that You would hold me precious!
I bow before You, aware of Your inexhaustible love.
Whatever strength I have I owe to You.
If only the self-sufficient could yield to You,
how much easier, happier, quieter their souls would be!
Your tasks—especially I—are works in progress.
But I trust wholeheartedly, Lord, that You
who started all these varied works in motion,
will guide each carefully to the goals You hoped for
when You called us out of nothingness into now.

Hymn
Take my life and let it be
Consecrated, Lord to Thee;
Take my moments and my days,
Let them flow in ceaseless praise.

Take my hands and let them move
At the impulse of Thy love.
Take my feet, and let them be
Swift and beautiful for Thee.

Take my voice and let me sing
Always, only, for my King.
Take my lips and let them be
Filled with messages from Thee.

Take my silver and my gold,
Not a mite would I withhold;
Take my intellect and use
Ev'ry pow'r as Thou shalt choose.

Take my will, and make it Thine,
It shall be no longer mine;
Take my heart, it is Thine own,
It shall be Thy royal throne.

Take my love—my Lord, I pour
At Thy feet its treasure store;
Take myself—and I will be
Ever, only, all for Thee.

—FRANCES R. HAVERGAL

Reading

It may be true that Christianity would be, intellectually, a far easier religion if it told us [to confine ourselves to acts of penitence and adoration, and not try to "engineer" events by petitionary prayers]. And I can understand the people who think it would also be a more high-minded religion. But remember the psalm: "Lord, I am not high-minded." Or better still, remember the New Testament. The most unblushingly petitionary prayers are there recommended to us both by precept and example. Our Lord in Gethsemane made a petitionary prayer (and did not get what He asked for).

—C. S. LEWIS, *LETTERS TO MALCOLM*

Scripture

Jesus said, "All you have to do is knock, and my Father is ready and eager to open his door to you. He will not send those who ask away empty-handed. If you honestly seek him, he is ready to be found. Would any of you give your child a shingle when he asks for a piece of bread? Or would you set a live snake on her plate when she asks for a fish?

As weak as you are, you don't begrudge loving care to your own children. How much more will your Father, who suffers no weakness at all, abundantly and open-handedly care for you? In dealing with one another, here is a simple rule of thumb: Treat others the way you'd hope they'd treat you—respectfully, graciously, solicitously. Every page of the scriptures is distilled into this one sentence: 'You've got to be kind.'"

—MATTHEW 7:7–12

Closing
God, my Friend,
my assistance in your plans is,
   in the overall picture, infinitesimal.
But it's not nothing.
Amen.

✝ Evening

Presence
Great Friend,
the day dies down.
The pressures ease away.
Let me rest my head
 on Your strong shoulder.

Grace
Abba, it's so humbling and exalting that You appreciate me.

Psalm
How do we thank the Lord for . . . everything?
For the dark days that make us love the light,
the annoying rain that nourishes our food,
the forgiveness we could do nothing to deserve?
With the Giver of All there can be no *quid pro quo*.

The Lord has told us what He hopes from us:
to do what is just, to love with steadfastness,
to take Him more seriously than we take ourselves.
—MICAH 6:6–8

Hymn
I am Thine, O Lord, I have heard Thy voice,
And it told Thy love to me;
But I long to rise in the arms of faith,
And be closer drawn to Thee.

Draw me nearer, nearer, blessed Lord,
To the cross where Thou hast died;
Draw me nearer, nearer, blessed Lord,
To Thy precious, bleeding side.

Consecrate me now to Thy service, Lord,
By the power of grace divine;
Let my soul look up with a steadfast hope,
And my will be lost in Thine.

There are depths of love that I cannot know
Till I cross the narrow sea;
There are heights of joy that I may not reach
Till I rest in peace with Thee.

Closing
Holy Friend,
my thanks for the gift of this day
   and for Your sharing it with me.
Amen.

First Friday

✟ Morning

Presence
Great Friend,
help me find a balance
    between honest satisfaction with who I've become
    and a restlessness to become someone better.

Grace
Abba, when I become sluggish, shake me awake.

Psalm
"If the wayward turn their backs on evil ways
and merely turn around in My direction,
they will come alive again, abundantly,
their sins not only forgiven but forgotten.
Do you think I delight in sinners wasting away?"
says the Lord of All. "I made them to *live*!
Nor are the good immovably rooted in righteousness.
They can warp into pious prigs, judgmental, vain,
measuring their worth by others' wickedness.
Some say, 'The Lord's not fair! We've paid our dues!'
I? It is *you* who are unfair, squandering My gifts.
Do you think I made you merely to be un-bad?
Whoever is not busy growing is busy dying."
                      —Ezekiel 18:21–28

Hymn
Thou art indeed just, Lord, if I contend
With thee; but, sir, so what I plead is just.
Why do sinners' ways prosper? and why must
Disappointment all I endeavour end?

Wert thou my enemy, O thou my friend,
How wouldst thou worse, I wonder, than thou dost
Defeat, thwart me? Oh, the sots and thralls of lust
Do in spare hours more thrive than I that spend,
Sir, life upon thy cause. See, banks and brakes
Now leavèd how thick! lacèd they are again
With fretty chervil, look, and fresh wind shakes
Them; birds build — but not I build; no, but strain,
Time's eunuch, and not breed one work that wakes.
Mine, O thou lord of life, send my roots rain.
                           —GERARD MANLEY HOPKINS, S.J.

Dedication
God, my Friend,
I offer You each moment of this day:
whatever comes—the unexpected challenges,
    diversions from my plans,
    the need-filled glance,
    the expectations and complaints,
    the being taken for granted,
    the slights and sleights-of-hand.
I'd be grateful if You could keep me aware of my pesky
        habits, like . . .
And, between us, perhaps we can enliven the spirits of
        those I live and work with, like . . .
Whatever else befalls,
    I trust we can cope with it,
    together.
Amen.

✚ Daytime

Presence
Great Friend,
help me penetrate the surfaces,
    to the substances of things,
    where You are.

Grace

Abba, temper my sense of injustice with forgiveness.

Psalm 130

Lord, from the welter of confusing voices, hear me.
Give me not just clear formulas but understanding.
Lord, if You keep a ledger of our stupidities,
who of us on earth could escape condemnation?
But You are incapable of mean-spiritedness,
for which we humble ourselves in gratitude.
I wait for Your light as sentinels watch for the dawn.
The Lord's coming scatters our groundless fears.
He will mend our mistakes with His mercy.

Hymn

The quality of mercy is not strain'd,
It droppeth as the gentle rain from heaven
Upon the place beneath: it is twice blest;
It blesseth him that gives and him that takes:
'Tis mightiest in the mightiest: it becomes
The thronèd monarch better than his crown;
His sceptre shows the force of temporal power,
The attribute to awe and majesty,
Wherein doth sit the dread and fear of kings;
But mercy is above this sceptred sway;
It is enthroned in the hearts of kings,
It is an attribute to God himself;
And earthly power doth then show likest God's
When mercy seasons justice. Therefore, . . .
Though justice be thy plea, consider this,
That, in the course of justice, none of us
Should see salvation: we do pray for mercy;
And that same prayer doth teach us all to render
The deeds of mercy.
                    —William Shakespeare, *The Merchant of Venice*

Reading

My cousin's husband who also teaches at Auburn came into the Church last week. He had been going to Mass with them but never showed any interest. We asked how he got interested, and his answer was that the sermons were so horrible, he knew there must be something else there to make the people come.

—FLANNERY O'CONNOR, *THE HABIT OF BEING*

Scripture

Jesus said, "Unless you do far better than justifying yourself with scrupulous adherence to the letter of the Law, like the Pharisees and legalists, and don't find its life-giving spirit with your hearts, you have little chance of entering the Kingdom. You've been told all your lives not to murder, or you will be caught and brought before a judge. Very few of you will even be tempted to do that. But I tell you now that, if you lose your temper with anyone, you have murdered them in spirit and in your heart, and are liable for that. If you thoughtlessly call someone 'Stupid!' or degrade anyone, you've forgotten that words can kill. So if you come to worship and suddenly remember a grudge you haven't let go, walk right out of the sanctuary, find that friend, and make peace. Only then come back and be worthy to deal with God. If someone brings a suit against you, right away, settle it between you, out of court, as two people who respect each other. The Law should give you both justice. I want the two of you to give one another mercy and forgiveness."

—MATTHEW 5:20–26

Closing

God, my Friend,
I ask only one gift:
   to be utterly honest with You
and with myself.
Amen.

✠ Evening

Presence
Great Friend,
today has been another gift.
I hope I've spent it well.

Grace
Abba, let me discover—and be—who I uniquely am.

Psalm
Don't deceive yourself that you've heard the word of
      God
because you've read it or heard someone speak the words.
You've heard it only when it governs your daily choices.
"Hearing" without acting is like glancing at yourself in a
      mirror,
and moments later you've forgotten your face, who you
      are.
If you see yourself reflected in the true law that frees,
you can't be distracted from who you're meant to be.
What you do will be who you are: blessed.
      —JAMES 1:22–25

Hymn
As kingfishers catch fire, dragonflies draw flame;
As tumbled over rim in roundy wells
Stones ring; like each tucked string tells, each hung bell's
Bow swung finds tongue to fling out broad its name;
Each mortal thing does one thing and the same:
Deals out that being indoors each one dwells;
Selves—goes itself; *myself* it speaks and spells,
Crying *what I do is me: for that I came.*

I say more: the just man justices;
Keeps grace: that keeps all his goings graces;

Acts in God's eye what in God's eye he is—
Christ—for Christ plays in ten thousand places,
lovely in limbs, and lovely in eyes not his
To the Father through the features of men's faces.
—GERARD MANLEY HOPKINS, S.J.

Closing
Holy Friend,
whatever I am and can become
I entrust to You.
Amen.

First Saturday

✢ Morning

Presence
Great Friend,
because I am grateful,
    help me to be gracious.

Grace
Eema, Holy Spirit, quicken my heart and soul.

Psalm
Wisdom is radiant and never fades or fails.
Those who love Her see Her, though others can't.
At gifted times, She quickens the soul without calling.
Watch for Her early, and find Her sitting on your
        doorsill.
To crave Her is the first step toward understanding.
She walks the streets and byways searching for seekers,
and She opens Her Spirit to theirs as they're walking
        along.
Welcome Her at your door, and She will enter, grace-
        fully.

—WISDOM 6:12–17

Hymn
O God, early in the morning I cry to you.
Help me to pray
And to concentrate my thoughts on you:
I cannot do this alone.
In me there is darkness,
But with you there is light;
I am lonely, but you do not leave me;

I am feeble in heart, but with you there is help;
I am restless, but with you there is peace.
In me there is bitterness, but with you patience;
I do not understand your ways, but you know the way for
   me. . . .

Restore me to liberty,
And enable me so to live now
That I may answer before you and before humanity.
Lord, whatever this day may bring,
Your name be praised.

—DIETRICH BONHOEFFER

Dedication
God, my Friend,
I offer You each moment of this day:
whatever comes—the unexpected challenges,
   diversions from my plans,
   the need-filled glance,
   the expectations and complaints,
   the being taken for granted,
   the slights and sleights-of-hand.
I'd be grateful if You could keep me aware of my pesky
      habits, like . . .
And, between us, perhaps we can enliven the spirits of
      those I live and work with, like . . .
Whatever else befalls,
   I trust we can cope with it,
   together.
Amen.

✢ Daytime

Presence
Great Friend,
remind me that love is not just a feeling,

but an act of will, a commitment
that takes over when the feelings fail.

Grace
Abba, create in me a fearless heart.

Psalm 119
Blessed are those ruled by the Lord's law of love,
who walk in peace with God and one another.
His law radiates from all the works of His hands:
the predictable order of the vast dance of stars
and the exuberant surprise of fireflies and giraffes
model a law of love, dutiful yet whimsical.
His will works patiently, resolutely toward holy
        wholeness:
humankind in tune with one another and within each soul.
Lord, etch Your law of love into my heart and will,
as You've engraved majesty into snowy mountains,
and roses serve You with their brief show of beauty,
birds chortle hymns, badgers burrow blind,
and we? We serve You in the thickets of our wits,
the compassion of our hearts, the readiness of our hands.
May I never forsake the tasks with which You honor me.

Hymn
I fled Him, down the nights and down the days;
I fled Him, down the arches of the years;
I fled Him, down the labyrinthine ways
Of my own mind; and in the mist of tears
I hid from Him, and under running laughter.
Up vistaed hopes I sped;
And shot, precipitated,
Adown Titanic glooms of chasmed fears,
From those strong Feet that followed, followed after.
But with unhurrying chase,
And unperturbèd pace,

Deliberate speed, majestic instancy,
They beat—and a Voice beat
More instant than the Feet—
"All things betray thee, who betrayest Me."
                    —FRANCIS THOMPSON, "THE HOUND OF HEAVEN"

Reading

But the final word is love. At times it has been, in the words
of Father Zossima, a harsh and dreadful thing, and our very
faith in love has been tried through fire. We cannot love
God unless we love each other, and to love we must know
each other. We know Him in the breaking of bread, and
we know each other in the breaking of bread, and we are
not alone any more. Heaven is a banquet and life is a banquet, too, even with a crust, where there is companion-
ship. We have all known the long loneliness and we have
learned that the only solution is love and that love comes
in community. It all happened while we sat there talking,
and it is still going on.
                    —DOROTHY DAY, THE LONG LONELINESS

Scripture

Jesus said, "You've heard all your lives you should be loyal to
your friends but that it's understandable to hate those who've
hurt and angered you. Well, let me tell you now, I want you
to be kind to your enemies and genuinely pray for those
who've wounded you. That will bring out the best in you,
which is the Spirit of your Father in heaven. He doesn't
discriminate among those to whom he offers life-giving
rain—those who love him and those who ignore him or hate
him. Why should God be pleased that you're gracious to
the attractive, the appealing, those who are easy to feel af-
fection for? Even outright crooks do that! If you greet only
pleasant folks, is there some merit in that? Even unbeliev-
ers do that! You must be whole—all-embracing—as your
Heavenly Father is whole and all-embracing."
                    —MATTHEW 5:43–48

Closing
God, my Friend,
help me be as prodigal in my caring
   as You are.
Amen.

✛ Evening

Presence
Great Friend,
let me not measure my life
   in weeks, days, hours,
but by who I am becoming.

Grace
Abba, give me the gracious gratitude to yield to You.

Psalm
Haven't you been listening? Don't you understand?
God didn't create the world, then wander off!
He's tireless in His vigilance, unwearying in His care.
But He *understands*. How could He not? He made us.
He knows even youngsters in their prime grow tired.
He waits to energize each willing soul, patiently,
slowly infusing His life into them as they rest,
readying them to rise up on sun-bright wings, like eagles.
Lay down your burden awhile, and let God work,
kneading your soul, easing the aching stiffness away,
strengthening your resolve to strive again.
                        —Isaiah 40:28–31

Hymn
For all thy saints who from their labours rest,
Who thee by faith before the world confessed,
Thy name, O Jesus, be for ever blessed,
Alleluia! Alleluia!

The golden evening brightens in the west,
Soon, soon to faithful warriors cometh rest,
Sweet is the calm of paradise the blessed,
Alleluia! Alleluia!

But there breaks a yet more glorious day,
The saints triumphant rise in bright array,
The King of Glory passes on his way,
Alleluia! Alleluia!

From earth's wide bounds, from ocean's farthest coast,
Through gates of pearl streams in the countless host,
Singing to Father, Son, and Holy Ghost,
Alleluia! Alleluia!

—WILLIAM W. HOW (1823–97)

Closing
Holy Friend,
I place my life in Your hands,
just as Your Son did.
Amen.

Second Sunday

✢ Morning

Presence
Great Friend,
take me, as a potter takes clay,
and form me as You will.

Grace
Abba, smother all resistance in me.

Psalm
Offer yourselves as a living sacrifice to God.
Make your ordinary, workaday life a gift
and offer it to Our Father to transform.
This is the true worship you should offer Him.
Don't let what "everybody does" justify you.
Offer yourself to be changed, from inside out.
Don't lower yourself to everyone else's expectations,
but raise yourself to what God can do with you.
Then you will find what God intended you to be.
—ROMANS 12:1–2

Hymn
Batter my heart, three-person'd God; for you
As yet but knock; breathe, shine, and seek to mend;
That I may rise, and stand, o'erthrow me, and bend
Your force, to break, blow, burn, and make me new.
I, like an usurp'd town, to another due,
Labour to admit you, but O, to no end.
Reason, your viceroy in me, me should defend,
But is captived, and proves weak or untrue.
Yet dearly I love you, and would be loved fain,

69

But am betroth'd unto your enemy;
Divorce me, untie, or break that knot again,
Take me to you, imprison me, for I,
Except you enthrall me, never shall be free,
Nor ever chaste, except you ravish me.
—JOHN DONNE, *HOLY SONNETS XIV*

Dedication
God, my Friend,
I offer You each moment of this day:
whatever comes—the unexpected challenges,
　　diversions from my plans,
　　the need-filled glance,
　　the expectations and complaints,
　　the being taken for granted,
　　the slights and sleights-of-hand.
I'd be grateful if You could keep me aware of my pesky
　　　　habits, like . . .
And, between us, perhaps we can enliven the spirits of
　　　　those I live and work with, like . . .
Whatever else befalls,
　　I trust we can cope with it,
　　together.
Amen.

✢ Daytime

Presence
Great Friend,
Your Son came
to alchemize our ordinariness
into a gift worthy of You.

Grace
Abba, let me be no obstacle to your Light.

Psalm 116

Even when I was afflicted, I still believed
because I know the Lord is merciful and compassionate.
My heart is confident because the Lord returns my
     trust.
I will keep believing, even when I feel overwhelmed;
even when I feel no one is loyal, You are.
I am Your servant, Lord, as my mother was.
You have set me free to live, and I truly shall.
I offer You that life in grateful thanksgiving,
and I praise Your name as long as you give me
     breath.

Hymn

In the beauty of the lilies,
Christ was born across the sea,
With a glory in His bosom
That transfigures you and me;
As he died to make men holy,
Let us die to make men free,
While God is marching on.
    —JULIA WARD HOWE, "THE BATTLE HYMN OF THE REPUBLIC"

Reading

It is very dangerous to go into eternity with possibilities
which one has oneself prevented from becoming realities.
A possibility is a hint from God. One must follow it. In
every one there is latent the highest possibility, one must
follow it. If God does not wish it then let God prevent it,
but one must not hinder oneself. Trusting to God I have
dared, but I was not successful; in that is to be found peace,
calm, and confidence in God. I have not dared: That is a
woeful thought, a torment in eternity.
    —SØREN KIERKEGAARD, *JOURNALS*

Scripture

Jesus took Peter, James, and John apart from the others and led them up onto a high mountain. While they were watching, Jesus suddenly was utterly transformed right before their eyes, as if all he was inside suddenly erupted radiantly to the surface. His clothes went blinding white, purer than clouds or snow. From the brightness emerged Elijah, the prophet, and Moses, the great lawgiver, as if the fullness the prophets and the Law were conversing easily with him. Peter suddenly blurted out, "Rabbi, how wonderful! Let us set up three memorials here, one for you, one for Moses, one for Elijah!" He had no idea what he was saying, they were so terrified. Then a cloud shadowed them, and from the cloud came a Voice: "This is my Son! My Beloved! Listen to him!" In an instant, it was gone. The disciples rubbed their eyes and saw Jesus alone. Only Jesus. As they worked their way down the mountain, Jesus warned them to keep what they had seen secret, until he had risen from the dead. They obeyed, but they continued to puzzle over what rising from the dead might mean.

—Mark 9:2–10

Closing

God, my Friend,
if I can transform only myself,
I have made the world better.
Amen.

☦ Evening

Presence

Great Friend,
Your promise within me
    takes the edge off all my faults.

Grace
Abba, let me be humble enough to value myself as You do.

Psalm
If God is on our side, who can make us afraid?
Can you imagine anything more precious to God
than His eternal self-expression: His Son?
And yet He unhesitatingly handed over His Best Loved
to become as weak as we are, to be vilely slaughtered,
and (far more important) to be raised, defeating Death.
If God has gone to such extremes of love,
what else does God have to hold back from us,
whom He purchased at such a staggering price?
If God has given His very *Self* to acquit us,
whose condemnation has any weight at all?

—ROMANS 8:31–34

Hymn
I heard the voice of Jesus say,
Come unto Me and rest,
Lay down thou weary one, lay down,
Thy head upon My breast.
I came to Jesus as I was,
Weary and worn and sad;
I found in Him a resting place,
And He has made me glad.

—HORATIUS BONAR

Closing
Holy Friend,
Your presence here
enfolds all I am in Your peace.
Amen.

Second Monday

✢ Morning

Presence
Great Friend,
today I will meet my share of arrogant ignorance.
Make me tolerant, patient, unwavering—kind.

Grace
Abba, give me wisdom to know when challenging a fool is
a waste.

Psalm 79
Again, Lord, the heathen are in control.
They've overwhelmed our cities and feed on our minds
and try to seduce our children to their false gods.
Strengthen our wills to subvert their paganism.
Hear the groans of boredom from their willing prisoners.
Show us the ways to prove their promises false.
Grant us the love and patience to wear them down.
We're asking here for the souls of our children, Lord.

Hymn
I heard an Angel singing
When the day was springing,
"Mercy, Pity, Peace
Is the world's release."
Thus he sung all day
Over the new mown hay,
Till the sun went down
And haycocks looked brown.
I heard a Devil curse
Over the heath and the furze,

"Mercy could be no more,
If there was nobody poor,
And pity no more could be,
If all were as happy as we."
At his curse the sun went down,
And the heavens gave a frown.
Down pour'd the heavy rain
Over the new reap'd grain . . .
And Miseries' increase
Is Mercy, Pity, Peace.

—WILLIAM BLAKE

Dedication
God, my Friend,
I offer You each moment of this day:
whatever comes—the unexpected challenges,
    diversions from my plans,
    the need-filled glance,
    the expectations and complaints,
    the being taken for granted,
    the slights and sleights-of-hand.
I'd be grateful if You could keep me aware of my pesky
        habits, like . . .
And, between us, perhaps we can enliven the spirits of
        those I live and work with, like . . .
Whatever else befalls,
    I trust we can cope with it,
    together.
Amen.

✝ Daytime

Presence
Great Friend,
help me find ways
to share more abundant life.

Grace
Abba, open my mind, my heart, my hands.

Psalm 27
The Lord gives bountiful light and zest to my living!
With Him at my side, I fear no one and nothing.
I stride through mean-spirited scoffers with a serene
      heart.
I ask for only one thing from life:
to feel the presence of God in the house of my soul.
When God whispered, "Come to Me," I found my place.
If everyone I know and love were to abandon me,
the only One who counts will never forsake me. ᐧ
Lord, when I come to crossroads, help me choose.
I'm confident in God's extravagant goodness to me.
Trust in the Lord. I say it again: Trust in the Lord!

Hymn
Lord, teach me to be generous.
Teach me to serve you as you deserve;
to give and not count the cost;
to fight and not heed the wounds;
to toil and not seek for rest;
to labor and not ask for reward, except to know
that I am doing your will.

—IGNATIUS LOYOLA

Reading
Nature is, above all, profligate. Don't believe them when
they tell you how economical and thrifty nature is, whose
leaves return to the soil. Wouldn't it be cheaper to leave
them on the tree in the first place ? This deciduous business alone is a radical scheme, the brainchild of a deranged
manic-depressive with limitless capital. Extravagance! Nature will try anything once. This is what the sign of the
insects says. No form is too gruesome, no behavior too

grotesque. If you're dealing with organic compounds, then let them combine. If it works, if it quickens, set it clacking in the grass; there's always room for one more; you ain't so handsome yourself. This is a spendthrift economy; though nothing is lost, all is spent.

—ANNIE DILLARD, *PILGRIM AT TINKER CREEK*

Scripture

Jesus said, "Be understanding, merciful, kind, as your Father is understanding, merciful, kind. Try not to criticize or find fault or condemn others, unless you want God to treat you that way. Forgive, no matter how painful, as you trust God will forgive you. Make giving freely your way of life, and God will replenish what you have to offer others—not merely replenish but a far richer supply than before, till your hands can hardly hold it. God is infinitely eager to outmatch your generosity."

—LUKE 6:36–38

Closing

God, my Friend,
help me be as profligate in my giving
as You are.
Amen.

✣ Evening

Presence

Great Friend,
The seas are great, and my skiff is small.
Becalm the waves for awhile.

Grace

Abba, let me accept that a hope to be perfect is blasphemous.

Psalm 26

If it's not overly presumptuous of me, Lord,
let me wash my hands among the innocent.
Given what You gave me to start with, I've really tried—
despite my inborn, chosen, and unchallenged
        weaknesses—
to do Your will insofar as You've let me discern it.
I praise You in the midst of the assembly of Your people.

Hymn

That there must be virtue in imperfection,
for Man is imperfect,
and Man is a creature of God.
That there must be virtue in frailty,
for Man is frail,
and Man is a creature of God.
That there must be virtue in brilliance, followed by
        stupidity,
for Man is alternately brilliant and stupid,
and Man is a creature of God.
        —KURT VONNEGUT, JR., PLAYER PIANO

Closing

Holy Friend,
I trust you enough
that I know I can rest content.
Amen.

Second Tuesday

✟ Morning

Presence
Great Friend,
help me to make today
    not "just one more day."

Grace
Abba, guide me to use my freedom wisely.

Psalm 13
Lord, sometimes You feel very distant, silent,
as if You were trying to hide Yourself from me.
Above all, I need a sense of Your presence with me,
not with sure-fire answers but for Your validation.
Don't let the meek voices within me hold me back.
Don't let others' skewed ideas tempt me to back
            down.
I ground my soul in the surety of Your love.
I sing to You, Lord, because You've been so good to me.

Hymn
Amazing grace! How sweet the sound
That saved a wretch like me.
I once was lost but now am found,
Was blind but now I see.

'Twas grace that taught my heart to fear,
And grace my fears relieved,
How precious did that grace appear,
The hour I first believed.

Through many dangers, toils and snares
I have already come.
'Tis grace hath brought me safe thus far,
And grace will lead me home.

Must Jesus bear the cross alone
And all the world go free
No, there's a cross for everyone
And there's a cross for me.

Amazing grace has set me free,
To touch, to taste, to feel;
The wonders of accepting love,
Have made me whole and real.

—JOHN NEWTON (1807)

Dedication

God, my Friend,
I offer You each moment of this day:
whatever comes—the unexpected challenges,
　　diversions from my plans,
　　the need-filled glance,
　　the expectations and complaints,
　　the being taken for granted,
　　the slights and sleights-of-hand.
I'd be grateful if You could keep me aware of my pesky
　　　　habits, like . . .
And, between us, perhaps we can enliven the spirits of
　　　　those I live and work with, like . . .
Whatever else befalls,
　　I trust we can cope with it,
　　together.
Amen.

✤ Daytime

Presence
Great Friend,
I have only one purpose:
to be the self You would have me be.

Grace
Abba, let me be utterly honest with myself, about myself.

Psalm 50
The Lord comes in fire and calls the whole universe,
His whole creation, to judge your secret hearts.
"Listen," says the Lord. "I don't reprimand your
          sacrifices.
But do I *need* the food you deny yourself and offer Me?
All animals, cattle, and birds were Mine from the
          beginning.
Let giving thanks in your hearts be your gift to God
by living the decent lives which are My Law within you.
And you—you, whose lives are mere gilded piety!
Why do you interpret My will with such meticulous care
to others, while your own hearts are closed off to Me?
Give Me the gratitude of an upright life. That's enough."

Hymn
Jesus, joy of man's desiring,
Holy wisdom, love most bright;
Drawn by Thee, our souls aspiring
Soar to uncreated light.
Word of God, our flesh that fashioned,
With the fire of life impassioned,
Striving still to truth unknown,
Soaring, dying round Thy throne.

Through the way where hope is guiding,
Hark, what peaceful music rings;
Where the flock, in Thee confiding,
Drink of joy from deathless springs.
Theirs is beauty's fairest pleasure;
Theirs is wisdom's holiest treasure.
Thou dost ever lead Thine own
In the love of joys unknown.

—MARTIN JANUS (1661)

Reading

This is the one true joy in life, the being used for a purpose recognized by yourself as a mighty one; the being a force of nature instead of a feverish, selfish little clod of ailments and grievances, complaining that the world will not devote itself to making you happy. . . . I am of the opinion that my life belongs to the whole community and as long as I live it is my privilege to do for it whatever I can. . . . I want to be thoroughly used up when I die, for the harder I work, the more I live. I rejoice in life for its own sake. Life is no "brief candle" to me. It is a sort of splendid torch which I have got hold of for the moment, and I want to make it burn as brightly as possible before handing it on to future generations.

—GEORGE BERNARD SHAW,
"DEDICATORY LETTER," MAN AND SUPERMAN

Scripture

Jesus spoke to the crowds and his disciples. "There is little doubt that the official teachers of religion and the Pharisees know more about the Law than most others. For the most part, what they offer you is reliable, and you should let your own conscience be guided by their teachings. But don't pattern your external behavior on the way they act, because they don't practice what they preach. The truth doesn't get through their surfaces into their hearts. They pile ordinary people's backs with loads of strictures they aren't willing to carry themselves. They take great pleasure in showiness, gaudy vestments and outward signs of authority, preening in flattery from ordinary people. They expect to be seated in prominent positions at social affairs and at worship. They delight in being called 'my Master.' They are masters only in a middling sense. Don't let anyone call *you* 'Master,' because you are all equally brothers and sisters of one another and have only one ultimate Master, one Truth, whose authority is far greater than theirs. Be grateful to your earthly fathers, but remember you have only one ultimate Father in heaven. Don't any of you try to domineer over others' lives. You have only one exemplary leader, Christ. The greatest among you are those who serve without fanfare. Whoever becomes pretentious will be humbled. Whoever puts the needs of others first, will be truly great."

—MATTHEW 23:1–12

Closing
God, my Friend,
I accept the burden
You've given no other creature:
   the freedom to think.
Amen.

✦ Evening

Presence
Great Friend,
I am surrounded
by so much light and life,
pulsing unseen!

Grace
Abba, make me aware of You, lurking everywhere.

Psalm

What earthly suffering God calls on us to bear
could compare to the glory with which Christ surrounds
       it?
All creation is eagerly straining toward fulfillment!
But God reins it in, evolving it ever so slowly.
What sustains us meantime is hope that all creation
will one day slough off its enslavement to decay.
Right now, the whole universe strains like a mother in
       labor,
and God's Spirit within us groans to be set free.
We hope for what we do not see and wait in patience.
                  —Romans 8:18–23

Hymn

Throughout my whole life,
during every moment I have lived,
the world
has gradually been taking on light and fire for me,
until it has come to envelop me
in one mass of luminosity,
glowing from within. . . .
The purple flush of matter
fading imperceptibly
into the gold of spirit,
to be lost finally
in the incandescence
of a personal universe. . . .
This is what I have learned
from my contact with the earth—
the diaphany of the divine
at the heart of the glowing universe,
the divine radiating from the depths of matter:
a-flame!
       —Pierre Teilhard de Chardin, S.J., *The Divine Milieu*

Closing
Holy Friend,
let me rest
in the brightness of peace.
Amen.

Second Wednesday—
Saint Joseph

♱ Morning

Presence
Great Friend,
not "Oh, God. *Another* day,"
but "Oh, God! Another *day*!"

Grace
Abba, help me rely less hesitantly on Your word.

Psalm
God promised Abraham his children would possess the
      earth,
not for what Abraham did but because God chose to.
If God keeps trust based only on some mutual contract,
then our faith is meaningless and God's promises are
      bought.
This is a promise from the God who defies
      containment,
who turned nothing into everything, who quickens the
      dead,
not because we kept the rules but because God *loves* us!
True love is neither ignited nor smothered by sterile
      rules.
or legalisms, or nitpicking minds, or barren hearts.
Abraham believed and hoped, even when there was no
      reason,
even when the promises seemed impossible or would
      never come true.

He is our common father in faith, not for his worthy
      deeds,
but because he stood firmly on his trust in God's word to
      him.
                          —ROMANS 4:13–22

Hymn
God grant me the serenity,
To accept the things I cannot change,
The courage to change the things I can,
And the wisdom to know the difference.

Living one day at a time;
Enjoying one moment at a time;
Accepting hardship as a pathway to peace;
Taking, as you did, this sinful world as it is,
not as I would have it;
Trusting that you will make all things right
if I surrender to your will;
That I may be reasonably happy in this life,
And supremely happy with you forever in the next.
                        —REINHOLD NIEBUHR

Dedication
God, my Friend,
I offer You each moment of this day:
whatever comes—the unexpected challenges,
   diversions from my plans,
   the need-filled glance,
   the expectations and complaints,
   the being taken for granted,
   the slights and sleights-of-hand.
I'd be grateful if You could keep me aware of my pesky
      habits, like . . .
And, between us, perhaps we can enliven the spirits of
      those I live and work with, like . . .

Whatever else befalls,
   I trust we can cope with it,
      together.
Amen.

✤ Daytime

Presence
Great Friend,
of all creatures You challenge only us
to choose, without dumb certitude.
Steady me.

Grace
Abba, fill in the gaps in my trust.

Psalm 89
The Lord said, "I have made covenant with My servant
         David,
a promise that a descendant of his will be king forever.
My strength guarantees his enemies will never defeat
         him.
I will make him My first-born Son, consummation of My
         hopes.
Once and for all, I promise by My own holy name
I can never break covenant or take back one promise I
         give him.
His kingdom will be as steadfast as the stars of heaven."

Hymn
He leadeth me, O blessed thought!
O words with heavenly comfort fraught!
Whatever I do, wherever I be
Still 'tis God's hand that leadeth me.

He leadeth me, he leadeth me,
By his own hand he leadeth me;
His faithful follower I would be,
For by his hand he leadeth me.

And when my task on earth is done,
When, by thy grace, the victory's won,
Even death's cold wave I will not flee,
Since God through Jordan leadeth me.
—JOSEPH HENRY GILMORE (1862)

Reading

Tell me, Joseph Carpenter, what it was like, from the beginning—to be such a woman's husband, father to such a boy, puzzling over quandaries no other man has faced, trusting at times when there was so little basis for it. When the girl you adored came to you with her preposterous story, and "something" indefinable convinced you her story was true, how confused and torn you must have been. Then the shame of being unable to provide her a proper place for the birthing, and, even worse, being uprooted like Abraham to travel by night into pagan Egypt to save this precious life—what kept you going? What burden was it to understand that this boy, whose schooling was no better than yours, had some insight into God of which no one else you knew was capable? How painful was it to see him grow away from you, forming a life so far beyond your comprehension? If you could share that with me, I think it would help me be a better parent myself.
—VICTOR STEELE, *INTERVIEWS WITH GOSPEL PEOPLE*

Scripture

When Jesus was twelve, his parents went to Jerusalem for the Passover feast, as they did every year. When they started their journey home, they had traveled a whole day before

each realized Jesus was not with the other or with any of
their relatives or friends. In panic, they hurried back toward Jerusalem and searched the city for him for three ago-
nizing days. Finally, they found him, sitting among the
eminent scholars, men they themselves would never have
dared even to approach, listening and asking questions, as
blithely as if he were their equal. Everyone there was astonished at the astuteness of his questions and his answers.
But his parents were not as impressed. "Son," his mother
said, shaking a bit, "why have you done this to us? Your
father and I have been at our wit's end searching everywhere for you." Jesus seemed puzzled. "But why were you
so worried that I was lost? Didn't you know I have to be
here in my Father's house, dealing with His affairs?" But
they had no notion what he was talking about. So Jesus
went back with them to Nazareth and lived obediently with
them. But his mother stored all these doings in her heart,
while Jesus grew in wisdom and stature, gaining esteem
with God and his neighbors.

—LUKE 2:41–51

Closing
God, my Friend,
give me the simple trust
to set free
    whatever I claim to love.
Amen.

✛ Evening

Presence
Great Friend,
in Your presence
    I don't find all the answers,
but everything "feels right."

Grace
Abba, make me see that heaven has already begun.

Psalm 84
How lovely and peaceful is the home You dwell in, Lord,
a place where I can sing out the joy in my grateful heart!
Even sparrows and swallows are welcome to build their nests
and raise their hatchlings in the niches of Your altars,
joining their twitterings with our humble songs of praise.
As we come in pilgrimage, You are not only our goal but
     our guide.
You walk with us through the lonesome valleys making
the dry gullies brim with pools of fresh rain.
And as we work our way up the last mountain curve,
there You are! God Almighty, welcoming us!
One day in Your presence is better than an opulent life.
It's a privilege merely to stand at Your gates and wait!
You honor us so far beyond our trifling worth.
Lord! How happy are those you trust in You!

Hymn
Swing low, sweet chariot,
Comin' for to carry me home!

I looked over Jordan and what did I see,
Comin' for to carry me home!
A band of angels comin' after me,
Comin' for to carry me home!

Swing low, sweet chariot,
Comin' for to carry me home!

If you get there before I do,
Comin' for to carry me home,
Jes' tell my friends that I'm a'comin' too,
Comin' for to carry me home.

Swing low, sweet chariot,
Comin' for to carry me home!

I'm sometimes up and sometimes down,
Comin' for to carry me home,
But still my soul feels heavenly bound
Comin' for to carry me home!

Closing
Holy Friend,
it's so good
to feel at home.
Amen.

Second Thursday

✝ Morning

Presence
Great Friend,
as Our Lady welcomed Your Son
   into her inmost self,
conceive Your Son within me.

Grace
Abba, infuse Your aliveness into mine.

Psalm 139
Oh, God! Your care for me is too much to grasp!
You know when I sit, when I stand, the thoughts
I barely comprehend in my own mind.
You watch me walk, lie down, my every move.
You know what I'll say before my mouth forms words.
Wherever I look—ahead, behind, within,
I encounter You, watchful, loving, ready.
Such concern for such as me overwhelms my heart.
If I flew on the wings of morning, You'd be at my side!
You turn every fearsome darkness into sunlight!
You wove me in the warp of my mother's womb—
my limbs, my eyes, my heart, my inmost self.
I invite You, Lord, to enter the dwelling You made me.
I consign it back to You. There are no hiding places.
Reconstruct it as You will, for within this self
we will dwell together when Time no longer is.

Hymn
Wilt thou love God as he thee? then digest,
My soul, this wholesome meditation,

How God the Spirit, by angels waited on
In heaven, doth make His temple in thy breast.
The Father having begot a Son most blest,
And still begetting—for he ne'er begun—
Hath deign'd to choose thee by adoption,
Co-heir to His glory, and Sabbath's endless rest.
And as a robb'd man, which by search doth find
His stolen stuff sold, must lose or buy it again,
The Sun of glory came down, and was slain,
Us whom He had made, and Satan stole, to unbind.
'Twas much, that man was made like God before,
But, that God should be made like man, much more.
—John Donne, *Sonnet XV*

Dedication
God, my Friend,
I offer You each moment of this day:
whatever comes—the unexpected challenges,
    diversions from my plans,
    the need-filled glance,
    the expectations and complaints,
    the being taken for granted,
    the slights and sleights-of-hand.
I'd be grateful if You could keep me aware of my pesky
        habits, like . . .
And, between us, perhaps we can enliven the spirits of
        those I live and work with, like . . .
Whatever else befalls,
    I trust we can cope with it,
        together.
Amen.

✠ Daytime

Presence
Great Friend,
help me savor each precious moment,

and yet see each one, too,
in the light of your forever.

Grace
Abba, let me delude no one, especially myself.

Psalm
The Lord says, "Cursed are the self-sufficient,
who have no time or desire or need for Me.
They are like tumbleweeds in the arid wilderness,
dry, aimless, rootless, borne on the wind.
But blessed are those who place their trust in Me.
Like the trees of Eden, they're rooted in living waters.
Scorching winds can't fade their freshness,
and the fruit in their arms will yield forever.
Who can cut through the thickets of the human heart?
I, the One God, penetrate to the roots and know
what hearts truly are and not what they pretend."
—JEREMIAH 17:5–10

Hymn
Philosophers have measur'd mountains,
Fathom'd the depths of seas, of states, and kinds,
Walk'd with a staff to heav'n, and traced fountains:
    But there are two vast, spacious things,
The which to measure it doth more behove:
Yet few there are that sound them; Sinne and Love,

    Who would know Sinne, let him repair
Unto Mount Olivet; there shall he see
A man so wrung with pains, that all his hair,
    His skinne, his garments bloudie be,
Sinne is that presse and vice, which forceth pain
To hunt his cruell food through ev'ry vein.

Who knows not, let him assay,
And taste that juice, which on the crosse a pike

Did set again abroach; then let him say
 If ever he did taste the like.
Love is that liquour sweet and most divine,
Which my God feels as bloud; buit I, as wine.

—GEORGE HERBERT

Reading

The soul has to go on loving in the emptiness, or at least
to go on wanting to love, though only with an infinitesimal part of itself. Then, one day, God will come to show
himself to this soul and to reveal the beauty of the world
to it, as in the case of Job. But if the soul stops loving it
falls, even in this life, into something almost equivalent
to hell.

—SIMONE WEIL, *WAITING FOR GOD*

Scripture

Once upon a time there was a rich man. Call him Dives.
He lived for only one reason: to flaunt his fabulous wealth—
clothes, mansion, lavish meals. At his gate squatted a wretch
named Lazarus, encased in sores that the street curs came
and licked. He yearned just to eat the rich man's trash. But
instead he died and was carried into heaven to Abraham's
embrace. But Dives died, too, and was entombed in hell.
From those depths, he saw Lazarus cradled high above in
Abraham's arms. So he cried out in agony, "Father Abraham, pity me! Send your Lazarus with just a single drop of
water to touch my burning lips!" But Abraham said, "Son,
during your life, you gorged yourself while Lazarus lay
empty at your doorstep. Now he is full, and you are drained.
And there is between us an impassable abyss." "Then, Father, send him to my five brothers to warn them against
this miserable place!" Abraham said, "They have Moses
and the prophets. Let them listen to them." Dives pleaded,
"But if someone came back from the *dead*, they'd listen and
change!" Abraham smiled ruefully. "If they shut their ears

to Moses and the prophets, they would ignore even one
risen from the dead."

—LUKE 16:19–31

Closing
God, my Friend,
remind me that
    the quiet voices of the past
    are most often wiser
    than the loudest in the present moment.
Amen.

✝ Evening

Presence
Great Friend,
re-enliven the youth in me,
    the wonder, the jubilance, the awe.

Grace
Abba, always remind me of what's truly important.

Psalm 137
By the rivers of this alien City we sat and wept,
remembering the simplicity of our true homeland.
We nested our silent harps in the twittering aspens,
for our captors jeered us to sing our homespun songs,
mocking our naive belief in a truer life,
a God who gives deeper purpose to our days.
Who could truly hear them in this raucous pit?
Lord, if I should ever forget my true home,
may my fingers wither, my tongue go numb.

Hymn
Try to remember the kind of September
When grass was green and grain was yellow

Try to remember the kind of September
When you were a young and callow fellow
Try to remember and if you remember
Then follow, follow, follow

Try to remember when life was so tender
And no one wept except the willow
Try to remember when life was so tender
And dreams were kept beside your pillow
Try to remember when life was so tender
When love was an ember about to billow
Try to remember and if you remember
Then follow, follow

Deep in December it's nice to remember
Although you know the snow will follow
Deep in December, it's nice to remember
Without a hurt, the heart is hollow
Deep in December, it's nice to remember
The fire of September, that made us mellow
Deep in December our hearts should remember
And follow . . . follow

—TOM JONES AND HARVEY SCHMIDT

Closing
Holy Friend,
I rest
   in the warmth
   of your wisdom.
Amen.

Second Friday

✟ Morning

Presence
Great Friend,
what a morning!
   For giving heart, and hope, and healing.

Grace
Abba, let me offer my life as freely as You gave it to me.

Psalm
Tell the tearful, "Take heart!" God is coming!
Blind eyes will fill with color and deaf ears with music!
Dry wells will brim over and wastelands will bloom.
And a Holy Road will open for God's faithful,
and at their head He will come strong and striding,
and all He has ransomed will return to their God-given
         home.
And in the face of their exuberant, joyful approach,
sorrow and sighing will flee forever in the winds.
                              —Isaiah 35:4–10

Hymn
I wonder as I wander,
out under the sky,
How Jesus the Savior
did come for to die,
For poor orn'ry people
like you and like I . . .
I wonder as I wander,
out under the sky.

                              —Appalachian Carol

Dedication
God, my Friend,
I offer You each moment of this day:
whatever comes—the unexpected challenges,
   diversions from my plans,
   the need-filled glance,
   the expectations and complaints,
   the being taken for granted,
   the slights and sleights-of-hand.
I'd be grateful if You could keep me aware of my pesky
      habits, like . . .
And, between us, perhaps we can enliven the spirits of
      those I live and work with, like . . .
Whatever else befalls,
   I trust we can cope with it,
   together.
Amen.

♱ Daytime

Presence
Great Friend,
so many I care for are in bondage—
   to things, to twisted truths, to hollow hopes.
Even if it costs me,
   help me find tactful ways to free them.

Grace
Abba, make me Your messenger.

Psalm
"Listen carefully," Jesus said. "I tell you what I *know*.
Yet if you quibble at down-to-earth truths,
how can I make you see eternal ones?
Which of your teachers has come from beyond this world?
Only one, the Son of Man, who speaks to the deaf.

Just as Moses raised a golden snake to focus belief,
So must the Son of Man be lifted up,
that all who believe his truth may have eternal life.
God loved all in this world so unreservedly
He surrendered His only Son, His inmost heart,
to assure your wholeness, fullness, abundant life."

—John 3:11–16

Hymn

When Israel was in Egypt's Land,
Let my people go,
Oppressed so hard they could not stand,
Let my people go.

Go down, Moses,
Way down in Egypt's Land.
Tell ol' Pharaoh,
Let my people go.

No more shall they in bondage toil,
Let my people go.
Let them come out with Egypt's spoil,
Let my people go.

Oh, come with Moses, you'll not get lost,
Let my people go.
He stretched his rod, we come acrost,
Let my people go.

Reading

Not like the brazen giant of Greek fame,
With conquering limbs astride from land to land;
Here at our sea-washed, sunset gates shall stand
A mighty woman with a torch, whose flame
Is the imprisoned lightning, and her name Mother of
    Exiles.

From her beacon-hand
Glows world-wide welcome; her mild eyes command
The air-bridged harbor that twin cities frame.
"Keep ancient lands, your storied pomp!" cries she
With silent lips. "Give me your tired, your poor,
Your huddled masses yearning to breathe free,
The wretched refuse of your teeming shore.
Send these, the homeless, tempest-tost to me,
I lift my lamp beside the golden door!"

—EMMA LAZARUS, *THE NEW COLOSSUS*

Scripture

"Once upon a time, there was a landowner who planted a vineyard, fenced it round, hollowed out a wine press and storage space for the wine. He leased the property to tenant farmers for a percentage and went off to tend his other holdings. Near vintage time, he sent servants to collect his share, but the tenants grumbled, 'We do all the sweating, and he sits back and collects.' So they thrashed one servant, stoned the second, and killed the third. When the owner heard, he sent even more servants, with the same results. At his wit's end, he sent his only son. 'Surely,' he thought, 'they don't dare harm my own son.' But the tenants were gleeful. 'Perfect!' they chortled. 'Kill the heir, and it's *all* ours!' So they hauled the son outside and murdered him. Now, can you try to guess what the owner would do when he rushed home after that news? Of course! He'll execute those killers and give the vineyard to honest workers who know what is theirs and what is his. I give you my word, the Kingdom of God will be taken from you who slaughtered God's messengers, even his Son, and be given to those who understand." The religious leaders knew he was vilifying them. They ached to arrest the arrogant upstart, but they were afraid of the ignorant mob who thought him a prophet—for the moment.

—MATTHEW 21:33–46

Closing

God, my Friend,
make me mindful always
    that all I have—even my shortcomings—
    are gifts.
Amen.

✢ Evening

Presence

Great Friend,
as this day gives way to night,
how grateful I am to have You with me.

Grace

Abba, let my living be one act of gratitude.

Psalm 145

Magnificent, munificent God! I will praise You forever!
Each age shouts Your great deeds from one to the next.
My soul stands in awe of Your wonders and Your story.
You are filled with tenderness and pity, slow to anger,
generous in kindness, endlessly eager to love.
You cup the elbows of all who stumble and raise them.
Whoever looks to You in hope will never feel alone.
The life in all that's living gives you praise!

Hymn

Father of night, Father of day,
Father, who taketh the darkness away,
Father, who teacheth the bird to fly,
Builder of rainbows up in the sky,
Father of loneliness and pain,
Father of love and Father of rain.

Father of day, Father of night,
Father of black, Father of white,

Father, who build the mountain so high,
Who shapeth the cloud up in the sky,
Father of time, Father of dreams,
Father, who turneth the rivers and streams.

Father of grain, Father of wheat,
Father of cold and Father of heat,
Father of air and Father of trees,
Who dwells in our hearts and our memories,
Father of minutes, Father of days,
Father of whom we most solemnly praise.

—BOB DYLAN

Closing
Holy Friend,
let me rest now
to be even more alive tomorrow.
Amen.

Second Saturday

✟ Morning

Presence
Great Friend,
what a joy!
To be alive another day!

Grace
Abba, help me see You beneath all the surfaces.

Psalm
Something that was before "is" had meaning—we saw!
We were there! Seeing it, hearing it, touching it with our
      hands!
The very Word of God who enlivens all that has "is"!
That life was made visible, palpable! The eternal in now!
We are here to witness we have touched the aliveness of
      God!
We declare it to you to share it with you:
the life shared by the Father and his Son, Jesus Christ!
We write this that your joy may be forever complete.
—1 JOHN 1:1–3

Hymn
The little cares that fretted me
I lost them yesterday
Among the fields, above the sea,
Among the winds at play,
Among the lowing of the herds,
The rustling of the trees,
Among the singing of the birds,
The humming of the bees.

The foolish fears of what might happen,
I cast them all away,
Among the clover-scented grass,
Among the new-mown hay,
Among the husking of the corn,
Where drowsy poppies nod,
Where ill thoughts die and good are born—
Out in the fields with God.
—ELIZABETH BARRETT BROWNING

Dedication
God, my Friend,
I offer You each moment of this day:
whatever comes—the unexpected challenges,
    diversions from my plans,
    the need-filled glance,
    the expectations and complaints,
    the being taken for granted,
    the slights and sleights-of-hand.
I'd be grateful if You could keep me aware of my pesky
        habits, like . . .
And, between us, perhaps we can enliven the spirits of
        those I live and work with, like . . .
Whatever else befalls,
    I trust we can cope with it,
    together.
Amen.

✚ Daytime

Presence
Great Friend,
if I have a single grudge left in my heart,
    help me smash its chains
    and be shed of it.

Grace

Abba, let me forgive as I am forgiven.

Psalm 103

Bless God, O my soul, from my very depths!
He forgives and forgets all our feeble offenses,
cures whatever within us is sickly and bent.
He snatches us back from the lip of the abyss
and reawakens the youthful vigor in our souls.
He hurls away our faults beyond all horizons.
Without Him, our merely human lives are chaff,
blooms of a day wafted off at the whim of the wind.
But He holds us in His merciful hands unto eternal life.

Hymn

Wilt Thou forgive that sin where I begun,
   Which was my sin, though it were done before?
Wilt Thou forgive that sin, through which I run,
   And do run still, though still I do deplore?
      When Thou hast done, Thou hast not done,
        For I have more.

Wilt Thou forgive that sin which I have won
   Others to sin, and made my sin their door?
Wilt Thou forgive that sin which I did shun
   A year or two, but wallowed in a score?
      When Thou hast done, Thou hast not done,
        For I have more.

I have a sin of fear, that when I have spun
   My last thread, I shall perish on the shore;
But swear by Thyself, that at my death Thy Son
   Shall shine as he shines now, and heretofore;
      And having done that, Thou hast done;
        I fear no more.
             —JOHN DONNE, *A Hymn to God the Father*

Reading

The captain said to me, when are you going to take the book? [Her nephew's confession.]

When I did not answer immediately, he said, I hope you will take it soon.

I said, out of some foolishness, will that help? . . .

There is a hard law, *mejuffrou*, he said, that when a deep injury is done to us, we never recover until we forgive.

—ALAN PATON, *TOO LATE THE PHALAROPE*

Scripture

Once upon a time there was a man with two sons. The younger boy said, "Father, give me my inheritance now while I'm young enough to enjoy it." So without a word, the father divided all he owned between the two. Almost immediately the younger lad packed up and took off for a faster life where he squandered his birthright. He was caught, penniless, in a famine and forced to hire himself out to feed swine. His belly yearned for the trash the pigs swilled down, but it was forbidden. So he saw his stupidity and resolved to go home. He even memorized an apology: "Father, I've sinned against God and you. I'm an unworthy son. But please, take me on as a field hand."

But his father was outside, peering into the distance for the boy, and when he saw him coming, he ran to his son, filled with joy, and embraced and kissed the lad before the boy could say a word. "Father," the boy began his apology, but his father didn't need that. "Quick!" he shouted to the servants, "Fetch the best robe! And a ring! And sandals! Kill the prize calf! We have to *rejoice*! My son who was dead is *alive* again!" And the whole village began to celebrate.

But the older, dutiful son, coming in sweating from the fields, heard the music and singing and asked what all this fuss was about. A servant said, "Your brother is back!" The older boy was furious and refused to go in, sulking outside.

His father came to beg him to come in, but he snapped, "I've slaved for you all my life, and you never *once* showed any gratitude. And this . . . this *bum*, this *leech* who spent half your life savings on *whores* comes crawling back and you give him a *party*?" But the father put his hand on his son's shoulder and said, "Son, I love you. Everything I have left I've given you. Can't you find it in your heart to be happy that your brother has come back to life again?"

—LUKE 15:11–32

Closing
God, my Friend,
forgiving sets free
   not only my offender
   but myself.
Amen.

✢ Evening

Presence
Great Friend,
thank You for the challenges of today.
I hope I proved worthy of Your trust.

Grace
Abba, let me cede the day to You.

Psalm
Lord, guide us with your crook to pasture for the night,
a quiet grassy glen in a grove of trees.
Who on earth—or beyond—can compare to You
for understanding our weakness and welcoming us
      home?
Like a mother, the one thing beyond Your infinite power
is nursing hard feelings or withholding Your infinite love.
You will stamp out our stupidities like a tramp's campfire

and hurl the filthy ashes to be consumed in the depths of
        the sea.
You are true to the promises You gave us in our making.
                                            —MICAH 7:14–20

Hymn
He's got the whole world in His hands,
He's got the whole world in His hands,
He's got the whole world in His hands.

He's got the little tiny baby in His hands,
He's got the little tiny baby in His hands,
He's got the whole world in His hands.

He's got you and me, sister, in His hands,
He's got you and me, brother, in His hands,
He's got the whole world in His hands.

He's got everybody here in His hands,
He's got everybody here in His hands.
He's got the whole world in His hands.

Closing
Holy Friend,
at the end of this day, this week,
I do rest—quiet, content, fulfilled
in Your hands.
Amen.

Thírd Sunday

✠ Morning

Presence
Great Friend,
Your purposes are clear.
But my mind and heart
   are still a bit befogged.

Grace
Abba, not my will but Your will be done.

Psalm
"I AM, the Lord, your only God, who set you free.
Do not use My name as a byword to vent your anger.
One day each week consecrate and concentrate to Me.
Honor the parents without whom you would not be.
You shall not kill or steal or degrade another's flesh.
Be scrupulously honest with your neighbors and yourself
Do not begrudge or envy your neighbors' success.
Do not lust after your neighbor's wife or children or
     goods."

—Exodus 20:1–17

Hymn
O God of earth and altar,
Bow down and hear our cry,
Our earthly rulers falter,
Our people drift and die;
The walls of gold entomb us,
The swords of scorn divide,
Take not thy thunder from us,

But take away our pride.
From all that terror teaches,
From lies of tongue and pen,
From all the easy speeches
That comfort cruel men,
From sale and profanation
Of honour and the sword,
From sleep and from damnation,
Deliver us, good Lord.
Tie in a living tether
The prince and priest and thrall,
Bind all our lives together,
Smite us and save us all;
In ire and exultation
Aflame with faith, and free,
Lift up a living nation,
A single sword to thee.

—G. K. Chesterton, "A Hymn"

Dedication

God, my Friend,
I offer You each moment of this day:
whatever comes—the unexpected challenges,
   diversions from my plans,
   the need-filled glance,
   the expectations and complaints,
   the being taken for granted,
   the slights and sleights-of-hand.
I'd be grateful if You could keep me aware of my pesky
      habits, like . . .
And, between us, perhaps we can enliven the spirits of
      those I live and work with, like . . .
Whatever else befalls,
   I trust we can cope with it,
   together.
Amen.

✠ Daytime

Presence
Great Friend,
Your Son's whole life is proof
 He didn't leave us the option
 to be shy, reserved, afraid.

Grace
Abba, shore up the weaknesses in me.

Psalm
Jews demand signs; Greeks want rational proof.
Despite them, we staunchly preach Christ crucified and
      reborn!
Jews call us gullible fools; Gentiles call us absurd.
But we, whose hearts He's grasped, feel the power
in the mangled Christ, the power and wisdom of God.
Human minds are too puny to capture His.
God's foolishness is too profound for human wisdom.
God's weakness is more powerful than human strength.
                              —1 CORINTHIANS 1:22–25

Hymn
A mighty fortress is our God,
A sword and shield victorious;
He breaks the cruel oppressor's rod
And wins salvation glorious.
The old evil foe,
Sworn to work us woe,
With dread craft and might
He arms himself to fight.
On Earth he has no equal.

No strength of ours can match his might!
We would be lost, rejected.

But now a champion comes to fight,
Whom God himself elected.
Ask who this may be:
Lord of Hosts is he!
Jesus Christ our Lord,
God's only son, adored.
He holds the field victorious.

—MARTIN LUTHER

Reading

You asked for a loving God: you have one. The great spirit you so lightly invoked, the "lord of terrible aspect," is present: not a senile benevolence that drowsily wishes you to be happy in your own way, not the cold philanthropy of a conscientious magistrate, nor the care of a host who feels responsible for the comfort of his guests, but the consuming fire Himself, the Love that made the worlds, persistent as the artist's love for his work and despotic as a man's love for a dog, provident and venerable as a father's love for a child, jealous, inexorable, exacting as love between the sexes.

—C. S. LEWIS, *THE PROBLEM OF PAIN*

Scripture

In spring, as Passover approached, Jesus went up to Jerusalem. He went into the Temple area, which was crammed, stall to stall, with bellowing oxen, foul-smelling sheep, screeching birds for sale to sacrifice, not to mention loan-sharks eager to fleece the rubes. Jesus was enraged at the sacrilege and braided a whip out of ropes and laid about him in fury, driving the exploiters out, scattering their animals, upending the loan-sharks' tables and scattering their plunder. "*Out!*" he roared. "Making my Father's house a cheap *bazaar!*" His friends thought of the scriptures: "Zeal for your house will devour me!" The enraged officials challenged him: "By what right do you *dare* to interfere, to cause this havoc?" Jesus pressed his broad hand against his heaving chest and growled, "Destroy *this* temple, and in three days I will raise it up again." The officials sneered, "This Temple took forty-six years to build! And you'll rebuild it in three days? Hah!" Only later, the disciples realized Jesus spoke of his own body. While Jesus was there for Passover, many came to believe. But Jesus was wary. He needed no advice about the duplicity of the human heart. He understood it all too well.

—JOHN 2:13–25

Closing
God, my Friend,
You gave me my voice.
Let me not be mute.
Amen.

♰ Evening

Presence
Great Friend,
accept this day in thanks
    for everything.

Grace
Abba, be my wise guide.

Psalm 61
Lord, sometimes I'm lost in a lonely landscape,
miles from nowhere, no landmarks in sight.
Take my hand, then, up the dizzying crags.
And when darkness falls, tent me under Your wings.
You've welcomed me into this life as Your guest,
given me freedom, space to move and breathe.
Help me to use my freedom as You would have me do.
Guide me, balance me along the razor ridges.
Make me both cautious and fearless as I make my way

always upward, even after I've slithered back down.
And I'm warmed by Your presence no matter how cold
      the climb.

Hymn
We sigh for human love, from which
A whim or chance may sever,
And leave unsought the love of God,
Tho' God's love lasts forever.

We seek earth's peace in things that pass
Like foam upon the river,
While steadfast as the stars on high,
God's peace abides forever.

Man's help, for which we long, gives way,
As trees in stormwinds quiver,
But mightier than all human need
God's help remains forever.

Turn unto Thee our wav'ring hearts,
O Thou who failest never;
Give us Thy love and Thy great peace,
And be our Help forever!

Closing
Holy Friend,
who could ask for anything more?
Amen.

Third Monday

✚ Morning

Presence
Great Friend,
in the week before us,
make me always aware of what is,
and just as aware of what ought to be.

Grace
Abba, help me face the truth, no matter how unpalatable.

Psalm 5
You, O God, hear me in the dawning day.
I fix my eyes on You. Help me keep them there.
You have no time for the canny, the cunning, the shrewd.
The braggart's boasts melt like frost under Your gaze.
You shun the deceitful, the seductive, the brutish.
Be at my side throughout this uncertain day.
Above all else, keep me honest with myself.
Let me tell myself no lies and, worse, believe them.
Surround me with Your truth, as with a shield.

Hymn
When to the sessions of sweet silent thought
I summon up remembrance of things past,
I sigh the lack of many a thing I sought,
And with old woes new wail my dear time's waste:
Then can I drown an eye, unused to flow,
For precious friends hid in death's dateless night,
And weep afresh love's long since cancell'd woe,
And moan the expense of many a vanish'd sight:

Then can I grieve at grievances foregone,
And heavily from woe to woe tell o'er
The sad account of fore-bemoaned moan,
Which I new pay as if not paid before.
But if the while I think on Thee, dear Friend,
All losses are restor'd and sorrows end.
—WILLIAM SHAKESPEARE, SONNET 30

Dedication
God, my Friend,
I offer You each moment of this day:
whatever comes—the unexpected challenges,
   diversions from my plans,
   the need-filled glance,
   the expectations and complaints,
   the being taken for granted,
   the slights and sleights-of-hand.
I'd be grateful if You could keep me aware of my pesky
     habits, like . . .
And, between us, perhaps we can enliven the spirits of
     those I live and work with, like . . .
Whatever else befalls,
   I trust we can cope with it,
     together.
Amen.

✚ Daytime

Presence
Great Friend,
let the eyes of my eyes be opened.
Let the ears of my ears understand.

Grace
Abba, make me sensitive to Your disguises.

Psalm 42–43

As the panting deer roams in search of a stream,
just so, O Lord, I search thirsting for You,
the energizing power within all that lives.
No one, O God, could see Your face and live,
but let me sense Your faithful presence near me,
beneath the skins and surfaces all around me,
for You dwell not far on high but at my fingertips.
Sensitize my soul to the God of gladness and joy!

Hymn

Oh, Jesus walked this lonesome valley.
He had to walk it by Himself;
'Cause nobody else could walk it for Him.
He had to walk it by Himself.

You got to walk this lonesome valley.
You got to walk it by yourself;
'Cause nobody else can walk it for you.
You got to walk it by yourself.

Oh, you must go and stand your trial.
You have to stand it by yourself;
'Cause nobody else can stand it for you.
You got to stand it by yourself.

Reading

Too late that I have loved, O Beauty, so ancient and so
new; too late have I loved you! Behold you were within
me, while I outside; it was there that I sought you, and a
deformed creature rushed headlong upon these things of
beauty which you have made. You were with me, but I was
not with you. They kept me far from you, those fair things
that, if they were not in you, would not exist at all. You
have called me, and have cried out, and have shattered my
deafness. You have blazed forth with light, and have shone

upon me, and you have put my blindness to flight! You have sent forth fragrance, and I have drawn in my breath, and pant after you. I have tasted you, and I hunger and thirst after you. You have touched me, and I have burned for your peace.

—AUGUSTINE OF HIPPO

Scripture

"I tell you the truth," Jesus said, "no prophet is appreciated by the people he cares about most, at home. But remember Elijah. When famine devastated all the lands around for three years and six months, there were many widows here in Israel, but Elijah was sent to only one—not here, but in the *pagan* town of Zarephath in Sidon. And when the prophet Elisha walked these hills, there must have been hundreds of lepers right here, but he cured only one— Naaman, a pagan *Syrian*."

When the people in the Nazareth synagogue heard that, they were enraged. They hurled him bodily out of the meeting place and dragged him to the edge of the cliff to cast him to his death. But Jesus set his face and passed through his furious neighbors unharmed.

—LUKE 4:24–30

Closing

God, my Friend,
I'm ready to go back "out there"
and meet You again.
Amen.

✛ Evening

Presence

Great Friend,
no matter how disjointed the day,
simplify my heart.

Grace
Abba, give me the confident serenity of a tightrope walker.

Psalm 4
Lord, when I ask for answers, if I don't quite understand
        them,
then give me patience to keep going until I do.
So many lug around their heavy hearts!
Trying to satisfy their hungry souls with wind,
griping their lives as if they had a right to live.
"More! More!" they bawl. "I can't get satisfaction!"
Restless because they miss the forever in now.
Lord, You give me such joy in an ordinary day!
In peace I lie down, resting secure in You.

Hymn
I know that my Redeemer lives;
What comfort this sweet sentence gives!
He lives, He lives, who once was dead;
He lives, my ever-living Head.

He lives triumphant from the grave,
He lives eternally to save,
He lives all-glorious in the sky,
He lives exalted there on high.

He lives, all glory to His name!
He lives, my Jesus, still the same.
Oh, the sweet joy this sentence gives,
I know that my Redeemer lives!

—SAMUEL MEDLEY

Closing
Holy Friend,
I offer You my day, lived.
I'll try my best again tomorrow.
Amen.

Third Tuesday—
The Annunciation

✠ Morning

Presence
Great Friend,
You sought her out
   not a gifted lady of Rome or Athens or Alexandria,
   but a young hill girl.
And You asked her *permission!*

Grace
Abba, with humble arrogance, I give You my permission.

Psalm
"All right," says the Lord, "if you demand a sign, here it is:
A girl inexperienced of men will bear a Son,
and she shall call him Immanuel—God Is With Us!"
—Isaiah 7:14

Hymn
Enough for him, whom cherubim
Worship night and day,
A breastful of milk,
And a mangerful of hay;
Enough for him, whom angels
Fall down before,
The ox and ass and camel
Which adore.

Angels and archangels
May have gathered there,

Cherubim and seraphim
Thronged the air:
But only his mother
In her maiden bliss
Worshipped the Belov'd
With a kiss.

What can I give him,
Poor as I am?
If I were a shepherd
I would bring a lamb;
If I were a wise man
I would do my part;
Yet what I can I give him—
Give my heart.

—CHRISTINA ROSSETTI

Dedication

God, my Friend,
I offer You each moment of this day:
whatever comes—the unexpected challenges,
    diversions from my plans,
    the need-filled glance,
    the expectations and complaints,
    the being taken for granted,
    the slights and sleights-of-hand.
I'd be grateful if You could keep me aware of my pesky
        habits, like . . .
And, between us, perhaps we can enliven the spirits of
        those I live and work with, like . . .
Whatever else befalls,
    I trust we can cope with it,
    together.
Amen.

✛ Daytime

Presence
Great Friend,
it's so fearsome
    to feel inadequate
    and yet chosen.

Grace
Abba, let me be willing to try.

Psalm
Mary said,
"My soul is exultant to bursting with praise of the Lord!
And my spirit leaps with joy in God, my Savior!
For He looked on me, the most insignificant of servants,
and there is no one more fortunate than I in the world!
For He who is mighty has done great things for me,
and holier is His name than any other, forever.
His mercy cascades upon those in awe of Him.
His mighty arm dismantles all arrogant boasts.
He's dragged the insolent from their thrones and lifted
        the lowly.
He summons hungry hearts to His royal feast,
and the complacent He dispatches, empty, away.
He has kept the timeless promise to His servant People
that He gave through Abraham to all, forever and
        beyond."

—Luke 1:46–55

Hymn
I sing of a maiden
That is matchless,
King of all kings
For her son she chose.
He came all so still

Where his mother was
As dew in April
That falls on the flower.
He came oh so still
Where his mother lay
As dew in April
That falls on the spray.
Mother and maiden
There was never one but she;
Well may such a lady
God's mother be.

Reading

I have no idea where I am going. I do not see the road
ahead of me. I cannot know for certain where it will end.
Nor do I really know myself, and the fact that I think that
I am following your will does not mean that I am actually
doing so. But I believe that the desire to please you does in
fact please you. And I hope I have that desire in all that I
am doing. I hope that I will never do anything apart from
that desire. And I know that if I do this you will lead me by
the right road though I may know nothing about it. Therefore will I trust you always though I may seem to be lost
and in the shadow of death. I will not fear, for you are ever
with me, and you will never leave me to face my perils alone.

—Thomas Merton, *Thoughts in Solitude*

Scripture

In the sixth month of Elizabeth's pregnancy, God sent the
angel Gabriel to Galilee in the north, to the village of
Nazareth, to a virgin named Mary, betrothed to a man
named Joseph, of David's house. He said to her, "Rejoice,
beloved of God! He is with you." The girl was utterly
stunned by this appearance, by his words and what they
could mean. But he said, "Peace, Mary. Have no fear at all.
You are most special to God. He's chosen you to conceive

and give birth to his Son whom you will name Jesus. He will be the great Son of the Most High. The Lord has readied the throne of David for him, and his rule over the People will have no end." Bewildered, Mary said, "How can this happen? I have never. . . . " But the angel answered, "God's own Spirit will possess you, and the bright cloud of God's presence will overshadow you. The child will be holy, the very Son of God. Your cousin, Elizabeth, who was barren is in her sixth month. See? Nothing is impossible for God!" Mary bowed her head. "I am God's servant. I don't understand. But I will do whatever God asks."

—Luke 1:26–38

Closing
God, my Friend,
You have merely to ask.
Amen.

✛ Evening

Presence
Great Friend,
in all this immensity,
who am I
that You should care for me?

Grace
Abba, let me be humble enough to accept being accepted.

Psalm
Even before the beginning, was the Word:
the Word was with God, and the Word was God.
He was one with God when nothing became everything,
and from him all-that-is derives its existence.
Nothing—*nothing*—exists except through him.
The aliveness within him is the light of humankind,

a light that banishes darkness and cannot be
       extinguished. . . .
The Word became flesh and came to dwell among us.
We have seen His radiance, the resplendence He shares
as the Father's only Son, fathomless grace and truth.

—JOHN 1:1–5, 14

Hymn
Salvation to all that will is nigh;
That All, which always is all everywhere,
Which cannot sin, and yet all sins must bear,
Which cannot die, yet cannot choose but die,
Lo! faithful Virgin, yields Himself to lie
In prison, in thy womb; and though He there
Can take no sin, nor thou give, yet He'll wear,
Taken from thence, flesh, which death's force may try.
Ere by the spheres time was created thou
Wast in His mind, who is thy Son, and Brother;
Whom thou conceivest, conceived; yea, thou art now
Thy Maker's maker, and thy Father's mother,
Thou hast light in dark, and shutt'st in little room
Immensity, cloister'd in thy dear womb.

—JOHN DONNE

Closing
Holy Friend,
for blessing my day,
through the Mother of Your Son,
thank You.
Amen.

Third Wednesday

✤ Morning

Presence
Great Friend,
knowing You, trusting You,
should make a recognizable difference in me.

Grace
Abba, let them see my freedom. Let them feel my joy.

Psalm
Listen: God sends you out to an alien people.
Their beliefs will be foreign to yours, as yours to them.
Puzzle them with the uprightness of your lives, your
        love, your joy.
Intrigue them to find a people pious but not priggish.
Make them wonder, "What do they know that I don't?
What's the secret that blends both duty and delight?
How do I meet a God so holy yet so near?"
Give those secrets away, but keep them in your hearts as
        well.
Cherish them, as you cherish the children you bequeath
        them to.
                                —Deuteronomy 4:5–9

Hymn
You may talk of my name as much as you please,
And carry my name abroad,
But I really do believe dat I'm a child o'God
As I walk in de heavenly road.
Oh, won't you go wid me, my friend,
For to keep our garments clean?

Come, my brutha, sistah, if you never did pray,
I hope you'll pray with me,
For I really believe you're God's chillun, too,
As we walk in de heavenly road.
Oh, won't you go wid me, my friends,
For to keep our garments clean?

Dedication

God, my Friend,
I offer You each moment of this day:
whatever comes—the unexpected challenges,
   diversions from my plans,
   the need-filled glance,
   the expectations and complaints,
   the being taken for granted,
   the slights and sleights-of-hand.
I'd be grateful if You could keep me aware of my pesky
     habits, like . . .
And, between us, perhaps we can enliven the spirits of
     those I live and work with, like . . .
Whatever else befalls,
   I trust we can cope with it,
   together.
Amen.

✢ Daytime

Presence

Great Friend,
others see You, worship You, understand You
   in ways far different from mine.
Open me so their friendship with You
   can enrich mine.

Grace

Abba, I dare not keep You to myself.

Psalm 147

How perfectly right it feels to sing the praises of God!
He who knows the number of stars and each one's name
yet has an eye for exiles, the broken, the poor.
He impregnates the clouds with rain to grow our food,
strews snow like a blanket and dew like liquid starlight,
scatters frost like breadcrumbs, and uncorks the winds.
He has power in plenty and no need of human force.
He takes no delight in our ferocity but in our
       faithfulness.
Our task is to bring Him to those who know Him not.

Hymn

We limit not the truth of God to our poor reach of
      mind—
By notions of our day and sect—crude partial and
      confined
No, let a new and better hope within our hearts be
      stirred
For God hath yet more light and truth to break forth
      from the Word.

Who dares to bind to one's own sense the oracles of
      heaven
For all the nations, tongues, and climes and all the ages
      given?
That universe, how much unknown! that ocean
      unexplored
For God hath yet more light and truth to break forth
      from the Word.

Eternal God, Incarnate Word, Spirit of flame and dove,
enlarge expand all living souls to comprehend your love;
and help us all to seek your will with wiser powers
      conferred

O God, grant yet more light and truth to break forth
    from the Word.
                                    —GEORGE RAWSON (1850)

Reading

[The goal] is simply a society controlled by the law of charity, the ethic of Christian love. . . . If charity is beautiful,
then lack of charity is correspondingly abominable. Not
only hatred, but even a careless disregard of one's neighbor
and his necessities is enough to deserve damnation. Those
condemned to hell in that terrible twenty-fifth chapter of
St. Matthew did not, apparently, really hate their needy
neighbors. They were simply too busy with their own selfish lives to care about them. Obviously, then, a mere lack
of concern for human suffering is itself damnable.
                                    —PAUL HANLY FURFY

Scripture

"Don't imagine for a minute I have come to abolish the scriptures that have guided our lives till now. No, no. Not to
demolish but to *deepen*, to lift it from scrolls and inscribe it
in the innermost recesses of your hearts. Listen hard. The
stars will fall and the earth disappear from under your feet
before one squiggle revealing God's will can disappear, not
till God's will is fulfilled. So, anyone who cheapens the most
minor expression of God's will, or induces others to flaunt
it, has yet to grasp what God's love is about. But whoever
fulfills God's will in love is worthy of his Kingdom."
                                    —MATTHEW 5:17–19

Closing

God, my Friend,
it would be so deadly dull
    if You'd made all of us identical.
Thank You for being so infinitely imaginative.
Amen.

✤ Evening

Presence
Great Friend,
Your love
　　turns the scars in my soul
　　to badges of honor.

Grace
Abba, let me exult in Your cleansing love.

Psalm
We believe, to the depths of our souls, God truly loves
　　　　us,
that we live *immersed* in God and God in us.
The proof is: We can face the Judgment unafraid
because even here and now we have become like
　　　　　Christ,
truly God's sons and daughters, as Christ has always
　　　　　been.
Genuine love can't even imagine fear.
Honest love blots out the *possibility* of fear,
because fear peers about, expecting punishment.
Whoever is afraid hasn't the vaguest idea of love.
　　　　　　　　　　　　　—1 JOHN 4:16–18

Hymn
When you walk through a storm
Hold your head up high
And don't be afraid of the dark.
At the end of the storm
Is a golden sky
And the sweet, silver song of the lark.
Walk on through the wind,
Walk on through the rain,
Though your dreams be tossed and blown.

Walk on, walk on with hope in your heart,
And you'll never walk alone!
You'll never walk alone.
> —Oscar Hammerstein II, "You'll Never Walk Alone"

Closing
Holy Friend,
it is such a gift
to be Your guest.
Amen.

Third Thursday

✜ Morning

Presence
Great Friend,
freedom is Your gift to me.
I would like to use it wisely.

Grace
Abba, with Your infinite patience, shape my soul.

Psalm
"If you would just listen to Me, if only once,
I will be your God, and you will be My people.
If you just live the way I tell you, you'd be happy!
Do they listen? No. Off they skedaddle,
following their noses wherever the whim takes them.
From the day the People left Egypt for freedom,
they have made My gift a diverting game.
For thousands of years I've sent them helpless
          messengers.
Each generation learns from the last to be worse!
Try. Oh, yes. You have to go on trying, as I have.
Just don't expect any immediate return. I don't.
What you will learn, surely, is patience, such as Mine."
                                        —JEREMIAH 7:23–28

Hymn
O Master, let me walk with Thee
In lowly paths of service free;
Tell me Thy secret, help me bear
The strain of toil, the fret of care.

Help me the slow of heart to move
By some clear, winning word of love;
Teach me the wayward feet to stay,
And guide them in the Godward way.

Teach me Thy patience; still with Thee
In closer, dearer company,
In work that keeps faith sweet and strong,
In trust that triumphs over wrong.

In hope that sends a shining ray
Far down the future's broad'ning way,
In peace that only Thou canst give,
With Thee, O Master, let me live.
—WASHINGTON GLADDEN

Dedication
God, my Friend,
I offer You each moment of this day:
whatever comes—the unexpected challenges,
   diversions from my plans,
   the need-filled glance,
   the expectations and complaints,
   the being taken for granted,
   the slights and sleights-of-hand.
I'd be grateful if You could keep me aware of my pesky
      habits, like . . .
And, between us, perhaps we can enliven the spirits of
      those I live and work with, like . . .
Whatever else befalls,
   I trust we can cope with it,
   together.
Amen.

✠ Daytime

Presence
Great Friend,
my demons have no horns or tails,
but they're demons nonetheless.

Grace
Abba, sensitize me to satanic subtleties.

Psalm
Paul addressed King Agrippa:

"I stormed into their meetings, torturing them to re-
cant this Jesus. My fury was so hot I went abroad to hound
them out. I was on my way to Damascus, commissioned by
the Temple, and at midday I and those with me were struck
down, blind! A voice said, 'Saul, Saul, why are you persecuting me? How do you stand it—bashing your soul against
the truth?' I groaned, sightless, reaching out, 'Who are you?
The Lord?' And the Lord said, 'I am Jesus, whom you are
persecuting! On your feet! I'm sending you as a witness to
this vision. I will protect you from the Jews and from the
foreigners to whom I send you. I send you to open their
eyes, so they turn from darkness to the light, from Satan to
God, and receive, through faith in me, forgiveness of their
sins and inherit their share of the Kingdom of Light.'"

—ACTS 26:11–18

Hymn
God rest you merry, gentlemen,
Let nothing you dismay,
Remember Christ our Savior
Was born on Christmas day,
To save us all from Satan's pow'r
When we were gone astray;

O tidings of comfort and joy,
Comfort and joy,
O tidings of comfort and joy.

Reading
Faustus: Who made thee?
Mephisto: God; as the light makes the shadow.
Faustus: Is God, then, evil?
Mephisto: God is only light,
And in the heart of the light no shadow standeth,
Nor can I dwell within the light of heaven
Where God is all.
Faustus: What are thou, Mephistopheles?
Mephisto: I am the price that all things pay for being,
The shadow on the world, thrown by the world
Standing in its own light, which light God is.
                            —DOROTHY L. SAYERS, *THE DEVIL TO PAY*

Scripture
When Jesus freed a man from the inner demon that had
rendered him mute, the man suddenly began to speak, and
the bystanders were stunned. But some of them sneered,
"Hah! Black magic! He does it with the power of Beelzebub,
lord of the flies, prince of the devils!" Other skeptics hesitated, asking for yet another sign from heaven to corrobo-
rate him. Jesus shook his head with a rueful smile at their
last-resort carping. "Wouldn't that be civil war?" he asked.
"The devil against himself?" He chuckled. "Satan can't last
long, then, if he works that stupidly. What's more, Solomon
taught your sons ways to outwit demons. Was Solomon a
devil? And all who followed his lead? I call them as my
witnesses, then. But," he said, pointing his finger at them,
"if in fact God himself gives me this power, then, my friends,
the Kingdom of God has just crept up on you!"
                            —LUKE 11:14–20

Closing
God, my Friend,
my mission is to liberate.
Amen.

✟ Evening

Presence
Great Friend,
take my hand.
I will go wherever You lead.

Grace
Abba, keep my will pliable, willing, ready.

Psalm 95
Come, let us shout the praises of the Lord, our God!
He is the one who carved the underground springs,
who sculpted the mountain peaks and spread out the sea.
Before His loving kindness we fall to our knees.
We are His People, the sheep of His flock.
"Harden not your hearts again," He cries,
"as your ancestors grumbled at Me in the wilderness!
Forty years they taxed Me with their fickle hearts.
If only you would yield, I could lead you to rest."

Hymn
Abide with me! fast falls the eventide;
The darkness deepens; Lord, with me abide!
When other helpers fail and comforts flee,
Help of the helpless, oh, abide with me.

Swift to its close ebbs out life's little day;
Earth's joys grow dim, its glories pass away;
Change and decay in all around I see;
O Thou who changest not, abide with me.

I fear no foe, with Thee at hand to bless:
Ills have no weight, and tears no bitterness:
Where is death's sting? where, grave, thy victory?
I triumph still, if Thou abide with me.

—HENRY LYTE

Closing

Holy Friend,
I trust in Your enduring presence
and rest there.
Amen.

Third Friday

✢ Morning

Presence
Great Friend,
false gods metastasize,
   so appealing, so unquestioned, so assumed.
At times, it feels pretty lonely out here.

Grace
Abba, even a solitary voice is better than none.

Psalm
Lord, let my sacrifice be denying my fear
to speak up in the face of bullies and charlatans.
I can't overcome them. They have too much power.
But I can resist them. I will never say, "My God,"
to any human handiwork or gilded dreams.
"If so, then I will cure My people," says the Lord.
"Forget their disloyalties and love them with all My
        heart.
They will be a fertile field again, abloom with lilies,
deep-rooted as the mighty cedars of Lebanon,
a People feasting to fulfillment on My bread and wine.
Let your wisdom be this: The Lord's ways lead to life,
and the upright will follow them, while fools will fall on
        their faces."

—Hosea 14:2–10

Hymn
I see his blood upon the rose
And in the stars the glory of his eyes,
His body gleams amid eternal snows,

His tears fall from the skies.
I see his face in every flower;
The thunder and the singing of the birds
Are but his voice—and carven by his power
Rocks are his written words.
All pathways by his feet are worn,
His strong heart stirs the ever-beating sea,
His crown of thorns is twined with every thorn,
His cross is every tree.

—JOSEPH MARY PLUNKETT (D. 1916)

Dedication
God, my Friend,
I offer You each moment of this day:
whatever comes—the unexpected challenges,
    diversions from my plans,
    the need-filled glance,
    the expectations and complaints,
    the being taken for granted,
    the slights and sleights-of-hand.
I'd be grateful if You could keep me aware of my pesky
        habits, like . . .
And, between us, perhaps we can enliven the spirits of
        those I live and work with, like . . .
Whatever else befalls,
    I trust we can cope with it,
    together.
Amen.

✟ Daytime

Presence
Great Friend,
if love's too easy,
it's unlikely to be love.

Grace
Abba, teach me to love the unlikable.

Psalm 81
I heard an unfamiliar whisper. "Listen!
It is I who lifted the burden from your back,
hurled off the yoke and bricks from your aching
       shoulder.
I heard your anguish in your chains and set you free!
I answered you in the thunder of Sinai and spoke My
       will.
Ah, My dear ones! Now you are free, beware
the earthy enticements and allure of hollow gods.
I am the Lord, your only God.
Do not exchange one enslavement for another.
If you freely choose the loving ways I've shown you,
your souls will fill to bursting with My joy!"

Hymn
Consider when thou art moved to be wroth,
He who was God and of all men the best,
Seeing Himself scorned and scourged both,
And as a thief between two thieves thrust,
With all rebuke and shame; yet from His breast
Came never sign of wrath or of disdain,
But patiently endured all the pain—
Think on the very lamentable pain,
Think on the piteous cross of woeful Christ,
Think on His blood beat out at every vein,
Think on His precious heart carved in twain;
Think how for thy redemption all was wrought,
Let Him not lose what He so dear hath bought.
              —PICO DELLA MIRANDOLA,
          TRANSLATED BY SAINT THOMAS MORE

Reading

Love people even in their sin, for that is the semblance of Divine Love, and is the highest love on earth. Love all of God's creation, the whole and every grain of sand of it. Love every leaf, every ray of God's light. Love the animals, love the plants, love everything. If you love everything you will perceive the divine mystery in things. Once you perceive it, you will begin to comprehend it better every day. And you will come at last to love the whole world with an all-embracing love.

—FYODOR DOSTOEVSKY, *THE BROTHERS KARAMAZOV*

Scripture

One of the legal experts respected what Jesus was saying and asked, "Which is the most important of all commandments?" Jesus answered, "This is the first: 'Listen! I am your one and only God, and you must love the Lord your God with all your heart, all your soul, all your mind, all your strength.' The second is this: 'Love your neighbors in the same way you care for yourself.' Every other commandment yields to those two." The scholar nodded. "Well said, Master. The way to fulfillment is simply that: to yield God all our loving, our living, our understanding, and our powers. And love one another as we would want to be loved ourselves. That is better than any other sacrifice." Jesus smiled at the man's insight and said, "My friend, you are not far from the Kingdom of God."

—MARK 12:28–34

Closing

God, my Friend,
loving is nowhere near as easy
as the songs would have us believe.
Amen.

✦ Evening

Presence
Great Friend,
Your Son, in His enfleshment,
hallows all things human.

Grace
Abba, let me sense the holiness in all You have made.

Psalm
People who had been walking in darkness have seen a
    great light!
A sunburst has blazed away all shadows and fear.
For unto us is born a Son, forever.
Wonderful! Counselor! The mighty God!
The everlasting Power! The Prince of Peace!
He assumes the throne of David and his Kingdom.
He will make it secure, becalmed, a place of peace.
    —Isaiah 9:1–2, 5–6

Hymn
Day is dying in the west,
Heav'n is touching earth with rest,
Wait and worship while the night
Sets her evening lamps alight
Through all the sky. Holy, holy, holy,
Lord God of Hosts!
Heav'n and earth are full of Thee!
Heav'n and earth are praising Thee,
O Lord, most high!

While the deepening shadows fall,
Heart of love, enfolding all,
Through the glory and the grace

Of the stars that veil Thy face,
Our hearts ascend.

—MARY LATHBURY

Closing
Holy Friend,
my heart and mind and body
rest—alive—in peace.
Amen.

Thírð Saturðay

✦ Morning

Presence
Great Friend,
again, *lentamente*.

Grace
Abba, let today be a day of peace—more or less.

Psalm
Come on, then! Let's get up and go back to the Lord.
Tears won't heal our wounded souls, but He will.
He'll straighten us out again, and in a day or two
we'll start to feel ourselves, and by the third
we'll feel like we've been born again, brand new!
If we strive toward Him, He'll come, as sure as dawn.
His love is like rain in Spring, making all things go on.
—Hosea 6:1–3

Hymn
Christ, whose glory fills the skies
Christ, the true, the only Light,
Sun of Righteousness, arise,
Triumph o'er the shades of night;
Dayspring from on high, be near,
Daystar, in my heart appear.

Visit then this soul of mine,
Pierce the gloom of doubt and grief;
Fill me, Radiancy divine,
Scatter all my unbelief;

More and more Thyself display,
Shining to the perfect day.

—CHARLES WESLEY

Dedication
God, my Friend,
I offer You each moment of this day:
whatever comes—the unexpected challenges,
    diversions from my plans,
    the need-filled glance,
    the expectations and complaints,
    the being taken for granted,
    the slights and sleights-of-hand.
I'd be grateful if You could keep me aware of my pesky
      habits, like . . .
And, between us, perhaps we can enliven the spirits of
      those I live and work with, like . . .
Whatever else befalls,
    I trust we can cope with it,
    together.
Amen.

✢ Daytime

Presence
Great Friend,
nothing can be so broken
You can't mend it.

Grace
Abba, make me content—but not too contented.

Psalm
God said to the weary Jeremiah, "Up!
Find your way to the potter's house, and there

I'll show you what I want you to understand."
So I went to the potter's place, and there he was,
working away at his whirling wheel. But
more than once the potter scowled and stopped.
He cocked his eye, this way and that, and his face
said, "No, that's not the pot I wanted at all."
Which can happen when you work with stuff as slippery
    as clay.
So he mashes the mud back to a shapeless lump
and, no matter the time, starts all over again.
"See?" said the Lord. "Does the potter ask the clay
permission to make it into a better pot?
I made you. Does that suggest any thoughts to you?"
—JEREMIAH 18:1–5

Hymn

I have no wit, no words, no tears;
My heart within me like a stone
Is numb'd too much for hopes or fears;
Look right, look left, I dwell alone;
I lift mine eyes, but dimm'd with grief
No everlasting hills I see;
My life is in the falling leaf:
O Jesus, quicken me.
My life is like a broken bowl,
A broken bowl that cannot hold
One drop of water for my soul
Or cordial in the searching cold;
Cast in the fire the perish'd thing;
Melt and remould it, till it be
A royal cup for Him, my King:
O Jesus, drink of me.
—CHRISTINA ROSSETTI, "A BETTER RESURRECTION"

Reading

I know things about you that no other person knows. You committed many more sins than people imagine; you performed many more miracles than people believe.

In order to mount to heaven, you used the floor of the Inferno to give you your momentum. "The further down you gain your momentum," you often used to tell me, "the higher you shall be able to reach." The militant Christian's greatest worth is not his virtue, but his struggle to transform into virtue the dishonor and malice within him.

—Nikos Kazantzakis, *St. Francis of Assisi*

Scripture

Jesus had a sense that more than a few of those listening to him were just a tad too self-satisfied and peered down their noses at common folks, so he told them this story: "Two men went into the Temple to pray, one was a worthy Pharisee, the other a contemptible tax gouger. The Pharisee struck a pose and said this prayer, to himself. 'Thank you, *God*, I'm not like *so* many others—leeching, crooked, lustful. But for the grace of God I'd be like that cringing *tax* collector back there. I fast *twice* a week. And I pay tithes on *every* shekel I make.' He purred contentedly, like a cat licking himself. Meanwhile, the tax man huddled in the shadows, ashamed even to look up at the altar. He struck his chest once with his fist. 'God,' he muttered, 'be merciful to me. I'm a sinner.' I tell you, my friends, that tax man went home friends with God, because he was honest—with himself and with God. The other didn't. Self-justification is its own impoverishment. Seeing yourself without pretenses is the first step toward the fulfillment God hopes for each of you."

—Luke 18:9–14

Closing

God, my Friend,
keep me growing,
   no matter the growing pains.
Amen.

♱ Evening

Presence

Great Friend,
I breathe easy because of You.

Grace

Abba, keep me astonished at Your kindness.

Psalm

Always be joyful in the Lord! I say it again:
Be joyful! Let all you meet see your good sense.
The Lord is so near; there's no need to worry about
     anything.
Bring your concerns to Him and put them in His hands,
letting your gratitude blot out all anxiety.
Then, the peace of God which defies understanding
will wrap your hearts and minds in the hands of Christ
     Jesus.
Finally, my friends, fill your hearts with all that's true,
all that's honorable, upright, pure—all we hold precious.
Focus your hearts and minds on all I taught you.
Then the God of peace will dwell in your souls.
         —PHILIPPIANS 4:4–9

Hymn

Come unto Me, ye weary,
And I will give you rest.
O blessed voice of Jesus,
Which comes to hearts opprest!

It tells of benediction,
Of pardon, grace, and peace,
Of joy that hath no ending,
Of love which cannot cease.

And whosoever cometh,
I will not cast him out.
O patient love of Jesus,
Which drives away our doubt,
Which, though we be unworthy
Of love so great and free,
Invites us very sinners
To come, dear Lord, to Thee!

—WILLIAM DIX

Closing
Holy Friend,
for no merit of mine,
You ennoble my life.
Amen.

Fourth Sunday

✠ Morning

Presence
Great Friend,
guide my heart, my mind, my hand
as we write my story.

Grace
Abba, let my living be a true message.

Psalm 23
The Lord is my shepherd. What more could I possibly
  need?
He beds me down in green pastures by untroubled
  waters.
When He's refreshed my soul, He rouses me
to walk the paths He's chosen just for me.
Even when I stumble blindly in dark valleys,
I have no fear, Lord, for You never leave my side.
Your strength is my strength, Your courage is my
  confidence.
You feast me in the face of those who call me fool.
You anoint me as Your royal messenger.
Who could ask for more than to do Your bidding?
Your goodness and kindness have become my bright
  shadows,
and I will dwell in Your house all the days of my life.

Hymn
Jesus, I know at least this is true:
I will follow You all of my days.
No one in history was ever like You,

and history itself is Your story.
Alpha and Omega, Your love is true,
And for eternity I'll share Your glory.

The center of all-that-is, my Savior,
God's story was readied for You,
Take my heart, my mind, my errant behavior,
and write what You will with my days.
For You are all that is noble and true.
You are God. I yield to Your ways.

Dedication
God, my Friend,
I offer You each moment of this day:
whatever comes—the unexpected challenges,
    diversions from my plans,
    the need-filled glance,
    the expectations and complaints,
    the being taken for granted,
    the slights and sleights-of-hand.
I'd be grateful if You could keep me aware of my pesky
        habits, like . . .
And, between us, perhaps we can enliven the spirits of
        those I live and work with, like . . .
Whatever else befalls,
    I trust we can cope with it,
        together.
Amen.

✝ Daytime

Presence
Great Friend,
if Your Son could work miracles
    with materials as unpromising as mud and spit,
surely You can work some minor miracles with me.

Grace

Abba, unlike Lucifer, let me serve by bearing Your light.

Psalm

Brothers and sisters, you once huddled in darkness,
but now you have *become* the light, in the Lord.
Live as his children, radiating his luminous life,
for light begets goodness, righteousness, truth.
Ponder over what would please our Lord.
Don't fritter away your days in killing time
or works one can do only under cover of night.
Let your honest light burn away the shaming surfaces
to see the inner goodness in what selfishness corrupts.
Awake, you sleepers! Come back to life from death!
And the light that rouses you to life is Christ, the Lord.

—EPHESIANS 5:8–14

Hymn

When I consider how my light is spent
E're half my days, in this dark world and wide,
And that one Talent which is death to hide,
Lodg'd with me useless, though my Soul more bent
To serve therewith my Maker, and present
My true account, lest he returning chide,
Doth God exact day-labour, light deny'd,
I fondly ask; But patience to prevent
That murmur, soon replies, God doth not need
Either man's work or his gifts, who best
Bear his milde yoak, they serve him best, his State
Is Kingly. Thousands at his bidding speed
And post o're Land and Ocean without rest:
They also serve who only stand and waite.

—JOHN MILTON, *On His Blindness*

Reading

Once upon a time there was a very bad girl. She raged
through the house like someone possessed. No one made

much effort to curb her. What good would it do? Since she was a year-and-a-half she'd been deaf, dumb, and blind. And her name was Helen Keller. As far as she knew, she was the only *person* in her safe, dark, little world. The rest were just bodies, getting in her way. Then one day there burst into her world a teacher named Annie Sullivan, half-blind herself and damned if she was going to just teach this little beast table manners. She was going to crack open that safe, dark, little world and let the great world come flooding in. For weeks, they wrestled and punched and clawed, until finally Helen relented a bit. She found she felt better clean than dirty. And always the puzzling game in the palm of her hand. Whenever she got her doll, four funny motions. Whenever she got a glass of water, five signs. That's all it was. Just a game. Then one day it happened. Helen's shoulder hit the pump, and she felt vibrations. She was curious. She hit the handle again and held out her hands. They were wet. Something inside was beginning to connect. And from her twisted mouth came the only word she could remember from her babyhood before the darkness, "*Wa-wa!*" Helen ran to Annie, and in her hand she spelled W-A-T-E-R. And then she spelled T-E-A-C-H-E-R. It had happened. It was the invasion. Helen Keller had discovered that things have names, that there was a whole *world* outside her darkness, other persons she could communicate to through the funny hand game. Poor frightened girl. She'd made the most liberating of all human discoveries. She'd discovered she wasn't alone.

—WILLIAM O'MALLEY, MEETING THE LIVING GOD

Scripture

His neighbors brought the blind man Jesus had cured with mud and his spittle to the Pharisees. They demanded to hear this trumped-up tale of his cure. "This man," he said, "he put wet clay on my eyes, I washed, and now I can see!" The holy men sneered, "Well, it can't be the work of God.

Not if this upstart pulls off his tricks on the sabbath!" Others took it up, "Hah! How could such a sinner do such wonders?" They grabbed the former blind man. "All right. You were the one he supposedly cured. What do you have to say about him?" The man said quite simply, "He's a prophet, of course." They railed at him: "How can this person be a prophet *and* a sinner?" The man shrugged. "Look. All I know is this. I was blind. Now I can see." The clerics were furious. "We speak in the name of Moses! In whose name does this charlatan speak?" The man sighed. "Can a man who is *not* of God give such a gift as opening the eyes of the blind?" They were speechless with rage, "You? You who were born reeking of sin are trying to teach *us?*" And they hurled him outside. Jesus found him and asked, "Friend, do you believe in the Son of Man?" The cured man squinted. "Who is he, sir, and I'll believe in him if *you* say so." Jesus smiled and said, "You're looking at him now, friend." The man opened a huge grin. "Then I do believe in him, sir!"

—JOHN 9

Closing
God, my Friend,
in the realm where You dwell,
I walk like someone blind.
Take my hand.
Amen.

✤ Evening

Presence
Great Friend,
without my trust in You.
my life is one blind stumble after another.

Grace
Abba, I believe. Help my unbelief.

Psalm
"I am the Light of the World," Jesus said.
"If you follow my will, you'll never walk in the dark.
You will carry within your soul the light of life.
I testify, I know, on my own behalf,
but my testimony is nonetheless true,
because I know whence I come and where I am going.
You judge by what you prove with your hands and minds.
But I have another Witness to the truth I claim.
My Father in heaven validates my every word."
—JOHN 8:12–18

Hymn
I never saw a moor,
I never saw the sea;
Yet know I how the heather looks,
And what a wave must be.

I never spoke with God,
Nor visited in Heaven;
Yet certain am I of the spot
As if a chart were given.
—EMILY DICKINSON

Closing
Holy Friend,
I place all my trust in You.
Amen.

Fourth Monday

✛ Morning

Presence
Great Friend,
so many of those You send me to
find learning and loving
less intriguing than
the weather reports.

Grace
Abba, we'll never win. But neither will we quit.

Psalm 31
Lord, in You I've sought and found my refuge.
Make my soul immune to the cynics' scorn.
Guide me through the enticing traps they spread
whose only gods are wallets and loins and bellies.
But You know—because You made me as I am—
their lies are truly tempting, and I am weak.
The sheer numbers of their believers is overwhelming,
and at times I feel the fool, shouting into a hurricane,
with no more chance of a hearing than a corpse.
So I beg not just for protection but for fearlessness,
conviction, a brave heart to carry on!

Hymn
I lift my soul to Him above,
And sing the angel's happy praise;
The song of life in joy of love
That men from earth to Heaven raise.

There's joy in Paradise for me,
Although a weary child of sin;
The penitent on Calv'ry's tree
May find the way to enter in.

My hopes are good, in Christ, the Lord;
On Him I rest my cares of heart;
He will so bridge the Heavenly Ford
To show the way ere I depart.

—MARCUS GARVEY

Dedication
God, my Friend,
I offer You each moment of this day:
whatever comes—the unexpected challenges,
    diversions from my plans,
    the need-filled glance,
    the expectations and complaints,
    the being taken for granted,
    the slights and sleights-of-hand.
I'd be grateful if You could keep me aware of my pesky
        habits, like . . .
And, between us, perhaps we can enliven the spirits of
        those I live and work with, like . . .
Whatever else befalls,
    I trust we can cope with it,
    together.
Amen.

✟ Daytime

Presence
Great Friend,
grafted into Your power,
I can do far more than I thought.

Grace
Abba, let me bring back souls from living death.

Psalm
Share your food with the hungry, your clothes with the
      poor.
Then your light will burst out in the darkness like
      dawn!
In healing the wounds of others, you will heal your own.
If you yourself cry out to God, He will whisper, "I'm
      here."
Grasp and hurl off the yokes of the weak and exploited.
Turn your clenched fist into a generous open hand,
and vindictive words to understanding forgiveness.
If you let afflicted hearts ignite your own,
your light will flare into a contagious fire,
and darkness for others will be for you like noon!
      —Isaiah 58:7–10

Hymn
Lord, enter into my inattentive eyes.
Let them see Your pain, regardless Your disguise.
Quicken my arms and hands to embrace
You, hiding beneath the grieving face.
When the hurt is beyond all words and skill,
Only a sacramental touching will.
Only the warmth of human flesh and bone
Says, "I'm helpless as you, but you're not alone."
      —Victor Steele

Reading
The cured man is no different from any other. It is a trivial
business unless you add the zest to the picture. That's how
I came to find writing such a necessity, to relieve me from
such a dilemma. I found by practice, by trial and error, that
to treat a man as something to which surgery, drugs and

voodoo applied was an indifferent matter; to treat him as material for a work of art made him somehow come alive for me.

—WILLIAM CARLOS WILLIAMS

Scripture

No sooner had Jesus returned to Cana in Galilee, where he'd turned the water into wine, than he was stopped by an official of the royal court in Capernaum, begging him to come to his home and cure his son, who was on the verge of dying. But Jesus was irritated with the constant nagging from officials, perhaps expecting just another trick. "Unless you people are bedazzled with miracles, you refuse to believe!" The official clutched his hands at his chest. "Sir. Please. My child. He's going to die." Jesus took a deep breath and said, "Go home, sir. Your son will live." Merely on Jesus' word, the man believed and rushed toward home, but while he was still far off, his servants met him. "The boy is well again!" The official grasped their hands, "When?" And they said, "The fever left him yesterday in mid-afternoon." It was at the very time Jesus had said, "Your son will live." And the man and all his household believed.

—JOHN 4:46–53

Closing
God, my Friend,
 remind me
 how healing simply caring can be.
Amen.

✢ Evening

Presence
Great Friend,
the day winds down,
and so do I.

Grace
Abba, remind me that my best is good enough.

Psalm
The Lord says, "I will cleanse the profanity from My
      Holy Name,
which even you, My people, have made a byword.
And the ungodly shall see My power in your goodness.
I shall bathe you in pure water and cleanse you of
      misdeeds.
I shall put My Spirit in you to guide your choices.
You will be My people, and I will be your God,
protecting you from everything that defiles.
—EZEKIEL 36:23–29

Hymn
It is a beauteous evening, calm and free,
The holy time is quiet as a nun
Breathless with adoration; the broad sun
Is sinking down in its tranquility;
The gentleness of heaven broods o'er the sea:
Listen! the mighty Being is awake,
And doth with his eternal motion make
A sound like thunder—everlastingly.
Dear Child! dear Girl! that walkest with me here,
If thou appear untouched by solemn thought,
Thy nature is not therefore less divine:
Thou liest in Abraham's bosom all the year,
And worship'st at the Temple's inner shrine,
God being with thee when we know it not.
—WILLIAM WORDSWORTH

Closing
Holy Friend,
let me leave all the day's concerns
safe in Your hands.
Amen.

Fourth Tuesday

✦ Morning

Presence
Great Friend,
Your world is so much more *alive*
   than we allow ourselves to see.

Grace
Abba, let me absorb the vigor and energy all around me.

Psalm 46
God is a place to withdraw awhile and grow strong.
We can stand fearless when the earth trembles and splits
      apart,
spewing liquid fire and hurling crags into the deep,
when the waters writhe and seethe in angry cliffs.
We serve the One who brought cosmos out of chaos.
When He raises His voice, pandemonium stops and
      listens.
He strides from camp to camp, cracking bows and spears,
and hurling all that kills to burn in the fire.
"Be *still!*" He cries. "And yield to the truth: I am God!"

Hymn
I caught this morning morning's minion, king-
   dom of daylight's dauphin, dapple-dawn-drawn
      Falcon, in his riding
  Of the rolling level underneath him steady air, and
      striding
High there, how he rung upon the rein of a wimpling wing
In his ecstasy! then off, off forth on swing,

As a skate's heel sweeps smooth on a bow-bend: the
    hurl and gliding
Rebuffed the big wind. My heart in hiding
Stirred for a bird,—the achieve of, the mastery of the
    thing!

Brute beauty and valour and act, oh, air, pride, plume,
    here
    Buckle! AND the fire that breaks from thee then, a
    billion
Times told lovelier, more dangerous, O my chevalier!

    No wonder of it: sheer plod makes plough down
    sillion
Shine, and blue-bleak embers, ah my dear,
    Fall, gall themselves, and gash gold-vermilion.
        —GERARD MANLEY HOPKINS, S.J., "THE WINDHOVER"

Dedication

God, my Friend,
I offer You each moment of this day:
whatever comes—the unexpected challenges,
    diversions from my plans,
    the need-filled glance,
    the expectations and complaints,
    the being taken for granted,
    the slights and sleights-of-hand.
I'd be grateful if You could keep me aware of my pesky
    habits, like . . .
And, between us, perhaps we can enliven the spirits of
    those I live and work with, like . . .
Whatever else befalls,
    I trust we can cope with it,
    together.
Amen.

✠ Daytime

Presence
Great Friend,
"there is more in heaven and earth
than is dream't of in our philosophy"—
or our science or our theologies.

Grace
Abba, rekindle in me the spirit of wonder.

Psalm 8
Lord, just speaking Your name empowers me!
Even in the songs of children, the burbling of babies,
Your life is spoken in defiance of unbelief.
I look to Your heavens, Your star-crusted cloak,
each flicker of fire fit into place by Your careful fingers!
In the face of such grandeur, what are we human beings,
soiled children of Adam, that You spare even a thought
            for us?
And yet You have made us only a whisper less than
            angels,
crowned us with Your glory, made us masters of Your
            earth,
given us minds to tame wild beasts and ourselves,
curiosity not merely to know what is but how it is made
and Your reason for bequeathing all-that-is to our care.
Oh, Lord, the power of Your presence blazes in all
            You've made!

Hymn
When I heard the learn'd astronomer,
When the proofs, the figures, were ranged in columns
            before me,
When I was shown the charts, the diagrams, to add,
            divide, and measure them,

When I sitting heard the learned astronomer where he
      lectured with much applause in the lecture room,
How soon unaccountable I became tired and sick,
Till rising and gliding out I wander'd off by myself,
In the mystical moist night-air, and from time to time,
Look'd up in perfect silence at the stars.

—WALT WHITMAN, LEAVES OF GRASS

Reading

It is almost impertinent to talk of the ascent of man in the presence of two men, Newton and Einstein, who stride like gods. Of the two, Newton is the Old Testament; it is Einstein who is the New Testament figure. He was full of humanity, pity, a sense of enormous sympathy. His vision of nature herself was that of a human being in the presence of something god-like, and that is what he always said about nature. He was fond of talking about God: "God does not play dice," "God is not malicious." Finally Neils Bohr one day said to him, "Stop telling God what to do." But that is not quite fair. Einstein was a man who could ask immensely simple questions. And what his life showed, and his work, is that when the answers are simple too, then you hear God thinking.

—DR. JACOB BRONOWSKI, THE ASCENT OF MAN

Scripture

Now in Jerusalem there was a pool called Bethesda, "House of Mercy," which has five porticos under which clustered sick people—blind, lame, paralyzed. One man had lived in pain, unable to walk for thirty-eight years, and when Jesus saw him, he was moved with compassion and said, "Do you want to be well again?" The man smiled weakly. "Sir, I am alone here. With no one to help me into the pool when the water stirs. By the time I get to the edge, there's no way to get through the crowd." Jesus smiled. "Get up, my friend. Take up your mat and walk." Slowly the man ached to his feet, his face beaming, and he sauntered about like a child dancing. But it happened to be the sabbath, and some pious Jews stopped the man as he was walking home. "Stop! You're forbidden to carry a sleeping mat on the sabbath!" The cured man grinned sheepishly. "But the man who cured me said, 'Roll up your mat and walk around.' So I did!" They snapped, "This man who told you to do this. Who was he?" The man didn't know; Jesus had disappeared into the crowd. But when the man ran into Jesus later, he went back and told those who had scolded him that the man had been Jesus. And from that day, the Jewish leaders began to watch his every move.

—JOHN 5:1–16

Closing
God, my Friend,
keep the hungers of my mind alive—
    and humble.
Amen.

✢ Evening

Presence
Great Friend,
my thanks,
for this palace of wonders.

Grace
Abba, let me rejoice that I have a place in Your plans.

Psalm
You who are thirsty, come! Come to the waters!
No need to pay for sustenance for the soul!
It's yours! Free! How can you merit or pay
for what God gives to all, no matter their worthiness?

Why do you waste your wages on what can't satisfy?
Come to Me! You merely need to listen to live.
Seek food for your bellies and answers for your hungry
        minds,
but I am here to satisfy the hungers of your hearts.
—Isaiah 55:1–3

Hymn

And as His Essence all the world pervades
Naught in Creation is, save this alone.
Upon the waters has He fixed His Throne,
This earth suspended in the starry space,
Yet what are seas and what is air? For all
Is God, and but a talisman are heaven and earth
To veil Divinity. For heaven and earth,
Did He not permeate them, were but names;
Know then, that both this visible world and that
Which unseen is, alike are God Himself,
Naught is, save God: and all that is, is God.
And yet, alas! by how few is He seen,
Blind are men's eyes, though all resplendent shines
The world by Deity's own light illumined,
O Thou whom man perceiveth not, although
To him Thou deignest to make known Thyself;
Thou all Creation art, all we behold, but Thou,
The soul within the body lies concealed,
And Thou dost hide Thyself within the soul,
O soul in soul! Myst'ry in myst'ry hid!
Before all wert Thou, and are more than all!
—Farid al-Din Attar

Closing

Holy Friend,
becalm my soul.
Amen.

Fourth Wednesday

✠ Morning

Presence
Great Friend,
rather than try to encompass Your infinite sea,
I will float, contented,
happy it has no ending.

Grace
Abba, You are my soul's sustenance.

Psalm
"Behold, the time is ripe! Here is My word.
I have formed you to be a covenant for My people.
Restore ravaged lands. Break down the walls of prisons.
Shout to those in darkness, 'Come out into the light!'
Pity them, slake their thirst in crystal waters.
I will open highways so all who wish can come home
from wherever they are all over the earth.
Let the heavens resound with delight! Let the earth
        exult!
Let the forested mountains tremble and jump for joy!
You thought I had forgotten, turned My back, deserted
        you.
Can a mother forget the infant suckling at her breast?
No, no! I have engraved your names in the palms of My
        hands."

—Isaiah 49:8–16

Hymn
I am, O anxious one. Don't you hear my voice
surging forth with all my earthly feelings?

They yearn so high, that they have sprouted wings
and whitely fly in circles round your face.
My soul, dressed in silence, rises up
and stands alone before you: can't you see?
Don't you know that my prayer is growing ripe
upon your vision as upon a tree?
If you are the dreamer, I am what you dream.
But when you want to wake, I am your wish,
and I grow strong with all magnificence
and turn myself into a star's vast silence
above the strange and distant city, Time.

—RAINER MARIA RILKE

Dedication
God, my Friend,
I offer You each moment of this day:
whatever comes—the unexpected challenges,
   diversions from my plans,
   the need-filled glance,
   the expectations and complaints,
   the being taken for granted,
   the slights and sleights-of-hand.
I'd be grateful if You could keep me aware of my pesky
      habits, like . . .
And, between us, perhaps we can enliven the spirits of
      those I live and work with, like . . .
Whatever else befalls,
   I trust we can cope with it,
   together.
Amen.

✤ Daytime

Presence
Great Friend,
Your creative Word is everywhere:

in Your universe,
in the ways You have made all things,
in Your Book,
in Your Eucharist,
in me.

Grace
Abba, help me fulfill my promise—my potential and my word.

Psalm
The Lord said to Abram, "My son, set aside all fears.
I have promised you a great reward, on My word."
Abram *wanted* to believe, but it had taken so long.
"Lord," he said, "what use are Your promised rewards
when You have left me childless? Without a son,
I must leave all You've given me now to a man of my
        household."
"No," God said sternly. "Such a one will not be your
        heir.
I've promised your heir will be the issue of your own
        body."
"But, Lord. . . . " Abram hesitated. "Come," said the
        Lord
and led Abram outside his tent under the canopy of stars.
"Look up!" God said. "Just try to count those lights!
That many descendants will you have. You have My
        word."
So Abram, an upright man, put his faith in the promise.
—GENESIS 15:1–6

Hymn
By the road to the contagious hospital
under the surge of the blue
mottled clouds driven from the
northeast—a cold wind. Beyond, the

waste of broad, muddy fields
brown with dried weeds, standing and fallen

patches of standing water
the scattering of tall trees

All along the road the reddish
purplish, forked, upstanding, twiggy
stuff of bushes and small trees
with dead, brown leaves under them
leafless vines—

Lifeless in appearance, sluggish
dazed spring approaches—

They enter the new world naked,
cold, uncertain of all
save that they enter. All about them
the cold, familiar wind—

Now the grass, tomorrow
the stiff curl of wildcarrot leaf
One by one objects are defined—
It quickens: clarity, outline of leaf

But now the stark dignity of
entrance—Still, the profound change
has come upon them: rooted, they
grip down and begin to awaken
—William Carlos Williams, "Spring and All"

Reading

[George has just told his wife, Maggie, he is thinking of leaving her.]
Maggie: I didn't marry you because you were perfect. I didn't even marry you because I loved you. I married you

because you gave me a promise. That promise made up for your faults. And the promise I gave you made up for mine. Two imperfect people got married, and it was the promise that made the marriage.

George: Maggie . . . I was only nineteen.

Maggie: And when our children were growing up, it wasn't a house that protected them: and it wasn't our love that protected them. It was that promise.

—THORNTON WILDER, *THE SKIN OF OUR TEETH*

Scripture

Jesus said, "My Father works on the sabbath. So do I." The most inflexible Jews were intent on killing Jesus not merely for breaking the sabbath but because he spoke as if he had some privileged connection to God, and if God were his Father in some unique way. Jesus spoke with patience. "In all truth, the Son of God can do nothing by himself alone. The Son does what the Father does, because the Father loves his Son and has promised to be with me. You will see him do wonders far greater than anything I have done. The Father gives life and forgiveness to anyone he chooses, and therefore so does his Son. Whoever refuses respect to the Son refuses respect to his Father. I tell you solemnly, whoever listens to my words and believes in the One who has sent me, has found the secret: eternal life, fulfillment, God's purpose for them. By myself I can do nothing. I can judge only as I am told to judge."

—JOHN 5:17–24, 30

Closing

God, my Friend,
In Your all-surrounding Word,
I trust.
Amen.

✛ Evening

Presence
Great Friend,
my living is so much richer
since You dared me
to let You in.

Grace
Abba, fill me with amazement at all I take for granted.

Psalm
We carry around this splendid message of light and
       freedom
in the unpretentious clay pots of our ordinary lives,
and the power burning within us is God's, not our own.
We've been battered about, but our souls are at peace.
We see no way out of the maze, but we're never
       dismayed.
We're cast down but never broken. There's life in us
       yet!
As we were joined in Christ's death, we're reborn to new
       life,
so that all we suffer now are insignificant deaths.
The scripture says, "I believed, therefore I spoke,"
so, too, we believe, therefore we are forced to speak,
that the grace of God can brim over and enliven all
       peoples.
Though our nature's flesh suffers, our souls are daily
       renewed,
readying themselves for the eternal weight of glory.
Our visible life is brief. Our invisible selves are forever.
       —2 Corinthians 4:7–18

Hymn

I got a robe,
You got a robe,
All God's Children got a robe;
When I get to Heaven,
Gonna put on my robe,
Gonna shout all over God's Heav'n.

Heav'n, Heav'n,
Ev'rybody talkin' 'bout
Heav'n ain't agoin' there,
Heav'n, Heav'n,
Gonna shout all over God's Heav'n.

I got a song,
You got a song,
All God's Children got a song;
When I get to Heaven,
Gonna put on my song,
Gonna shout all over God's Heav'n.

—HARRY THACKER BURLEIGH (1921)

Closing

Holy Friend,
I need a bit of time
to catch my breath.
Amen.

Fourth Thursday

✣ Morning

Presence
Great Friend,
the only thing necessary
    for the triumph of evil
is for good men to do nothing.
—Edmund Burke (1729–97)

Grace
Abba, let me stand up to be counted.

Psalm
I saw the Lord, seated on a lofty throne,
the train of His robe spilled over the whole sanctuary.
Six-winged angels burned in the air above Him,
shouting to one another, "Holy, holy, holy!
Lord of All Armies—in heaven, in the stars, and on
        earth!
His glory radiates from whatever wherever it is!"
The place trembled with their shouting and billowed
        with smoke.
I cried, "I am *lost*! A man of unclean lips!
And my eyes have seen the King, the Lord of Hosts!"
Then one of the fiery folk flew toward me
with a white-hot coal from the altar and touched my lips.
"See?" the angel said. "Your unworthiness has no
        meaning."
God thundered, "Whom shall I send? Who will go for
        Us?"
And I heard myself say, "Here I am. Send me."
—Isaiah 6:1–9

Hymn

First they came for the Jews
and I did not speak out
because I was not a Jew.
Then they came for the Communists
and I did not speak out
because I was not a Communist.
Then they came for the trade unionists
and I did not speak out
because I was not a trade unionist.
Then they came for the Catholics,
and I did not speak out
because I was not a Catholic.

Then they came for me
and there was no one left
to speak out for me.

—PASTOR MARTIN NIEMÖLLER

Dedication

God, my Friend,
I offer You each moment of this day:
whatever comes—the unexpected challenges,
   diversions from my plans,
   the need-filled glance,
   the expectations and complaints,
   the being taken for granted,
   the slights and sleights-of-hand.
I'd be grateful if You could keep me aware of my pesky
     habits, like . . .
And, between us, perhaps we can enliven the spirits of
     those I live and work with, like . . .
Whatever else befalls,
   I trust we can cope with it,
   together.
Amen.

✛ Daytime

Presence
Great Friend,
I want to learn to say,
"Here I stand. Thus far. No further."

Grace
Abba, make me adaptable but aware when compromise
becomes capitulation.

Psalm 106
The spineless People made a golden calf
and fell to their knees before it, shouting its praises,
yielding their glory to a symbol of brute coupling.
They forgot the God who'd made them an image of
      Himself,
rescued them from bondage where they'd been like beasts,
given them power to know and love Him freely,
trusted them to be His, as He was their faithful God.
Thwarted yet again by His own wilful creatures,
the Lord resolved to be shed of them, once for all,
to start over as He had in Noah's time.
But Moses, fearless with the authority God had given
      him,
stood up to the Lord Himself and begged for mercy.
And God relented, hoping they would learn to be brave.

Hymn
Onward, Christian soldiers, marching as to war,
With the cross of Jesus going on before.
Christ, the royal Master, leads against the foe;
Forward into battle see His banners go!

Like a mighty army moves the church of God;
Brothers, we are treading where the saints have trod.

We are not divided, all one body we,
One in hope and doctrine, one in charity.

Onward then, ye people, join our happy throng,
Blend with ours your voices in the triumph song.
Glory, laud and honor unto Christ the King,
This through countless ages men and angels sing.

—SABINE BERING-GOULD

Reading

And touching our Society, be it known to you that we have made a league—all the Jesuits in the world, whose succession and multitude must overreach all the practice of England—cheerfully to carry the cross you shall lay upon us, and never to despair your recovery, while we have a man left to enjoy your Tyburn, or to be racked with your torments, or consumed with your prisons. The expense is reckoned, the enterprise is begun; it is of God; it cannot be withstood. So the faith was planted: So it must be restored.

If these my offers be refused, and my endeavours can take no place, and I, having run thousands of miles to do you good, shall be rewarded with rigour, I have no more to say but to recommend your case and mine to Almighty God, the Searcher of Hearts, who send us his grace, and see us at accord before the day of payment, to the end we may at last be friends in heaven, when all injuries shall be forgotten.

—EDMUND CAMPION, S.J.

Scripture

"You sent messengers to John, and he testified to me. But I'm not submitting myself to your human judgment, nor do I have need of human testimony. For a while, John was a torch by which you found your way. But, great as John was, my testimony is more deeply rooted than his. My Father has been testifying for me since the very beginning, and the proof of that is in the mission He gave me to perform. No matter your protestations, you don't really hear his voice or see his will. The proof of *that* is your refusal to accept the one he's sent you. Oh, you bury your noses in scriptures, searching like miners for the final truth. But all the scriptures point to me, and you refuse to accept the truth of life from me. Listen. I am *not* looking for human glory. Surely not praise from such as you, who have no honest love of God within you. You've rightly placed your hopes in Moses. Well, it's Moses who will rise up and accuse your short-sightedness. If you really believed him, you would really believe me. But you don't *truly* believe in Moses, do you? If you did, you wouldn't close your minds to me."

—JOHN 5:31–47

Closing
God, my Friend,
if I yield to everything,
I stand for nothing.
Amen.

✦ Evening

Presence
Great Friend,
life is surely a serious business,
but why do so many make it gruesome?

Grace
Abba, let me serve you with a truly light heart.

Psalm
Seize the day! Eat your food with gusto!
Drink your wine with a light and gladsome heart.
The God who made them takes pleasure in your
          happiness.

Let your clothing reflect the joy within.
Relish the life you have with the spouse you love.
Do your work with a great heart and be proud of it.
Each day is precious because it's precarious.
One day it will be too late to say, "I love you."
—ECCLESIASTES 9:7–10

Hymn

When I play on my fiddle in Dooney,
Folk dance like a wave of the sea;
My cousin is priest in Kilvarnet,
My brother in Mocharabuiee.
I passed my brother and cousin:
They read in their books of prayer;
I read in my book of songs I bought at the Sligo fair.
When we come at the end of time
To Peter sitting in state,
He will smile on the three old spirits,
But call me first through the gate;
For the good are always the merry,
Save by an evil chance,
And the merry love the fiddle,
And the merry love to dance:
And when the folk there spy me,
They will all come up to me,
With "Here is the fiddler of Dooney!"
And dance like a wave of the sea.
—WILLIAM BUTLER YEATS, "THE FIDDLER OF DOONEY"

Closing

Holy Friend,
let my gratitude for life
be obvious.
Amen.

Fourth Friday

✚ Morning

Presence
Great Friend,
how do I offer a richer life
    to people who don't want to be bothered?

Grace
Abba, keep me persistent and confident.

Psalm
Let us lay traps for the upright. They make us uneasy,
carping against the way we live our lives,
that we go against the ways of our simple parents.
Do they have some special insight into God
and His mysterious plans for what ordinary humans
        should be?
Let us taunt and test their haughty convictions, then!
They claim God is their Father. Let's just see if that's
        true.
If God *is* their Father, He'll protect them, won't He?
Yes, let us put their gentle patience to the test.
and God will hold them upright—so they claim.

—WISDOM 2:12–22

Hymn
Suns have set and suns will rise
Upon many gloomy lives;
Those who sit around and say:
"Nothing good comes down our way."
Some say: "What's the use to try,
Life is awful hard and dry."

If they'd bring such news to you,
This is what you ought to do.

Let no trouble worry you;
Keep cool, keep cool!
Don't get hot like some folk do,
Keep cool, keep cool!
What's the use of prancing high
While the world goes smiling by.
You could win if you would try,
Keep cool, keep cool.

—MARCUS GARVEY

Dedication
God, my Friend,
I offer You each moment of this day:
whatever comes—the unexpected challenges,
    diversions from my plans,
    the need-filled glance,
    the expectations and complaints,
    the being taken for granted,
    the slights and sleights-of-hand.
I'd be grateful if You could keep me aware of my pesky
        habits, like . . .
And, between us, perhaps we can enliven the spirits of
        those I live and work with, like . . .
Whatever else befalls,
    I trust we can cope with it,
        together.
Amen.

✢ Daytime

Presence
Great Friend,
cleanse my mind and heart

of any resentfulness
that you are God, and I am not,
that you have ways and purposes
I will never fathom.

Grace

Abba, I treasure my curious mind. Help me concede its limits.

Psalm

"Who is this, subjecting My intentions to his ignorance?
Let Me ask you questions, and I'll allow you to enlighten
      Me.
Where were you when I laid the foundations of the
      earth?
Who decided its dimensions? Do you know?
Were you there when all the morning stars shouted for
      joy?
Who pent up the seas when they roared to engulf the
      earth?
Who said, 'No further! Here will your proud waves
      break'?
Have you ordered the dawn to tint the earth like a gown?
Do you know the gatekeepers at the Shadow darker than
      death?
If you do know, you must be very old by now."
—Job 38:1–14, 17, 21

Hymn

So humble things Thou has borne for us, O God,
Left'st Thou a path of lowliness untrod?
Yes, one, till now; another Olive-Garden,
For we endure the tender pain of pardon,—
One with another we forbear. Give heed,
Look at the mournful world Thou has decreed.
The time has come. At last we hapless men

Know all our haplessness all through. Come, then,
Endure undreamed humility: Lord of Heaven,
Come to our ignorant hearts and be forgiven.
—ALICE MEYNELL, *"VENI CREATOR"*

Reading

Dogma can in no way limit a limitless God. The person
outside the Church attaches a different meaning to it than
the person in. For me a dogma is only a gateway to con-
templation and is an instrument of freedom and not of re-
striction. It preserves mystery for the human mind. Henry
James said the young woman of the future would know
nothing of mystery or manners. He had no business to limit
it to one sex.
—FLANNERY O'CONNOR, *THE HABIT OF BEING*

Scripture

As Jesus spoke in the Jerusalem Temple, some bystanders
whispered to one another, "Isn't this the one they want to
knock off? But he's right there, talking away, and none of
them stands up to him. You think the powers-that-be caved
in? That they think he's the Messiah?" Another scoffed.
"Look, we know where this one *comes* from. Everybody
knows, when the Messiah shows up, he'll be from some-
place nobody ever heard of."

Jesus snapped at them. "You have it all figured out,
haven't you? You know who I am because you know where
I come from. You've been told who the Messiah is 'allowed'
to be? But I came at the will of Someone greater than your
scholars, and he who sent me is incapable of untruth. For
all your certitudes, for all that you know *about* him, you
simply don't know *him*. But I do know him because my
very being is in him who sent me."

They wanted to arrest him on the spot, but it was not
yet the right time, and no one dared lay a hand on him.
—JOHN 7:25–30

Closing

God, my Friend,
it is sheer presumption
   that I should "forgive" You,
but with all my heart
   I do.
Amen.

✦ Evening

Presence

Great Friend,
the day's had its ups and downs.
Thank you for making the journey with me.

Grace

Abba, grant me the serenity to take one step at a time.

Psalm 37

Don't let the smug get you all heated up
or envy the ones who "made it" the easy way.
Their "fifteen minutes of fame" are merely that,
Someone else is ready and eager to take their places.
Open yourself to God. Live at peace with Him
in your home. He knows what needs to be done.
Stay quiet with Him. Nurture peace in your soul,
and don't fret about those who elbow you out of their way.
Bridle your resentments. Snuff out your rage.
Frustration has no effect on them, only you.
It's the honest, down-to-earth folks who'll inherit the earth.

Hymn

Let there be peace on earth,
and let it begin with me.
Let there be peace on earth,
the peace that was meant to be.

With God as our Father,
brothers all are we,
Let me walk with my brother,
in perfect harmony.

Let peace begin with me,
let this be the moment now.
With every step I take,
let this be my solemn vow,

To take each moment and live each moment
in peace, eternally.
Let there be peace on earth,
and let it begin with me.

—JILL JACKSON AND SY MILLER (1955)

Closing
Holy Friend,
sufficient for the day
is the struggle thereof.
Amen.

Fourth Saturday

✟ Morning

Presence
Great Friend,
make me neither
too defensive,
nor too offensive.

Grace
Abba, teach me to be a clever subversive.

Psalm 7
Those who resent their indebtedness to You
are slyer than snakes when they challenge Your truth.
"Your book is a collection of fairy tales for simple minds,
Your religion a tangle of pharisaic rules,
Your leaders a gang of gilded hypocrites,
Your people no better than anyone else—or worse."
How can I help but admit we have our faults?
But at the core of our weakness is a message of freedom
        and joy!
Lord, give me the wits to confront their malice calmly.
Give me the patience to love them despite their spite.
Make me clever enough to trip them into their own
        traps,
not for vengeance but that the jolt might pull them up
        short and see.

Hymn
Creator Spirit, by whose aid
The world's foundations first were laid,
Come, visit every humble mind;

Come, pour Thy joys on humankind;
From sin and sorrow set us free
And make Thy temples worthy Thee.

O Source of uncreated light,
The Father's promised Paraclete,
Thrice holy Fount, thrice holy Fire,
Our hearts with heavenly love inspire;
Come and Thy sacred unction bring
To sanctify us while we sing.

—JOHN DRYDEN (1693)

Dedication

God, my Friend,
I offer You each moment of this day:
whatever comes—the unexpected challenges,
    diversions from my plans,
    the need-filled glance,
    the expectations and complaints,
    the being taken for granted,
    the slights and sleights-of-hand.
I'd be grateful if You could keep me aware of my pesky
        habits, like . . .
And, between us, perhaps we can enliven the spirits of
        those I live and work with, like . . .
Whatever else befalls,
    I trust we can cope with it,
    together.
Amen.

✠ Daytime

Presence

Great Friend,
when the truth
clearly challenges my certitudes,
make me go back and start over again.

Grace
Abba, remind me I'll never reach the horizon.

Psalm
For within Wisdom is a Spirit, intelligent and holy.
She is unique, seed-filled, subtle, lively, piercing,
untainted, lucid, invulnerable, openhanded, shrewd,
tolerant, understanding of all human weakness,
steadfast, imperturbable, penetrating all souls.
For Wisdom is faster than lightning. She is pure
and suffuses all things on earth and in heaven.
She is the breath of the power of God Himself,
the mirror reflecting His never-ending light.
She is the embodiment of God's goodness.
—WISDOM 7:22–26

Hymn
Yet all experience is an arch wherethro'
Gleams that untravell'd world, whose margin fades
For ever and for ever when I move.
How dull it is to pause, to make an end,
To rust unburnish'd, not to shine in use!
As tho' to breath were life. Life piled on life
Were all to little, and of one to me
Little remains: but every hour is saved
From that eternal silence, something more,
A bringer of new things; and vile it were
For some three suns to store and hoard myself,
And this gray spirit yearning in desire
To follow knowledge like a sinking star,
Beyond the utmost bound of human thought.
—ALFRED LORD TENNYSON, *ULYSSES*

Reading
I too think the intellectual should constantly disturb, should
bear witness to the misery of the world, should be provocative by being independent, should rebel against all hidden

and open pressure and manipulations, should be the chief doubter of systems, of power and its incantations, should be witness to their mendacity. For this reason, an intellectual cannot fit into any role that may be assigned to him. . . . An intellectual essentially doesn't belong anywhere; he stands out as an irritant wherever he is; he does not fit into any pigeonhole completely. . . . To a certain extent an intellectual is always condemned to defeat. He is like Sisyphus in that regard. . . . And yet in another, more profound sense the intellectual remains, despite all his defeats, undefeated— again like Sisyphus. He is in fact victorious through his defeats.

—VACLEV HAVEL, *DISTURBING THE PEACE*

Scripture

Some in the crowds were convinced. "Yes. He's a prophet" and "The Messiah!" But others were more than skeptical. "The Messiah? From Galilee? The books say the Christ will be a son of David, from Bethlehem." Those wanted to turn him over to the police, but they preferred to keep out of it. When the Temple guards reported back, the priests and Pharisees scowled. "Well? Where is he? Why haven't you brought him in?" The guards were shamefaced. "You . . . you don't understand, masters. No one has *ever* spoken the way this man does." The churchmen huffed in frustration. "So! He's got *you* under his spell, too? Your job is to carry out orders, not make such decisions. Has any of *us* endorsed this upstart? Any of the men who have devoted their *lives* to the Law? You were cowed by the ignorant rabble, who know *nothing* of the Law. Condemned by their own gullibility." But Nicodemus, one of their number who had met privately with Jesus, spoke up: "But our Law clearly forbids us to pass judgment on someone without first giving him a hearing." The rest shook their heads. "Unbelievable! *You* can't be one of these Galileans, too! All right. Go see for yourself. It's *impossible* for a prophet to come out of Galilee!"

—JOHN 7:40–52

Closing

God, my Friend,
be with me
as I swim against the tide.
Amen.

✠ Evening

Presence

Great Friend,
as You keep no scrupulous tally
   of what was right and wrong with today,
neither shall I.

Grace

Abba, let it be enough to know You care about me.

Psalm

Blessed be God, the Father of our Lord Jesus Christ,
who in His great love has given birth to living hope
in the resurrection of Christ which ends the power of
        death.
We share His heritage which can never be taken away.
No matter what comes, you are eternal, here and now.
Even gold will perish, but you will not.
Feel secure in your destiny: indescribable joy!
For Christ has assured that your lives are not in vain.
                                        —1 PETER 1:3–9

Hymn

I've reached the land of corn and wine,
And all its riches freely mine;
Here shines undimmed one blissful day,
For all my night has passed away.

O Beulah Land, sweet Beulah Land,
As on thy highest mount I stand,

O look away across the sea,
Where mansions are prepared for me,
And view the shining glory-shore,
My heav'n, my home for evermore!

My Savior comes and walks with me,
And sweet communion here have we;
He gently leads me by His hand,
For this is heaven's border-land.

—Edgar Page

Closing
Holy Friend,
make me daily more capable of joy
so I'm prepared for it forever.
Amen.

Fifth Sunday

✟ Morning

Presence
Great Friend,
our choices are never truly free
   unless we form them,
unblinking,
    in light of the total Truth.
And death is the most undeniable of truths.

Grace
Abba, make me unflinchingly honest.

Psalm
Those who judge only by pleasure and time
can't comprehend the hopes God has for them.
But your judgments, guided by the Spirit in you,
lead you step by step in an eternal light.
And if the immortal Christ dwells within you,
how could you ever stop living eternal life?
Even though the body that defines and encases your self
dies, all that makes you *you* can never perish,
because all you truly are is enlivened by God.
—Romans 8:8–11

Hymn
Death, be not proud, though some have called thee
Mighty and dreadful, for thou art not so;
For those, whom thou think'st thou dost overthrow,
Die not, poor Death, nor yet canst thou kill me.
From rest and sleep, which but thy pictures be,
Much pleasure, then from thee much more must flow,
And soonest our best men with thee do go,

Rest of their bones, and soul's delivery.
Thou'rt slave to Fate, chance, kings, and desperate men,
And dost with poison, war, and sickness dwell,
And poppy, or charms can make us sleep as well,
And better than thy stroke; why swell'st thou then?
One short sleep past, we wake eternally,
And Death shall be no more; Death, thou shalt die.
—JOHN DONNE, *HOLY SONNETS X*

Dedication
God, my Friend,
I offer You each moment of this day:
whatever comes—the unexpected challenges,
    diversions from my plans,
    the need-filled glance,
    the expectations and complaints,
    the being taken for granted,
    the slights and sleights-of-hand.
I'd be grateful if You could keep me aware of my pesky
        habits, like . . .
And, between us, perhaps we can enliven the spirits of
        those I live and work with, like . . .
Whatever else befalls,
    I trust we can cope with it,
        together.
Amen.

✟ Daytime

Presence
Great Friend,
help me to savor
    the time,
    the challenges,
    the people I love
while I have them.

Grace
Abba, let the inescapable fact of death put my priorities in true order.

Psalm
Thus says the Lord: "My people, I will open your graves
and lift you from death back into abundant life.
Then you will believe that I am truly the Lord,
when I crack open your tombs and you come striding
        forth.
O my people! I will put *My* Spirit in you, which cannot die!
I have promised. I will do it. On My word," says the Lord.
                                            —EZEKIEL 37:12–14

Hymn
[Death,] What will you have when you finally have me?
Nothing.
Nothing I have not already given
freely each day I spent
not waiting for you
but living
as if the shifting shadows of grapes
and fine-pointed leaves in the shelter
of the arbor would continue to tremble
when my eyes were absent
in memory of my seeing,
or the books fall open where I marked them
when my astonishment overflowed
at a gift come unsummoned, this love
for the open hands of poems,
earth fruit, sun soured grass, the steady
outward lapping stillness of midnight
snowfalls, an arrow of light waking me
on certain mornings with sharp wound
so secret that not even you
will have it when you have me.

You will have my fingers
but not what they touched. Some gestures
outflowing from a rooted being, the memory
of morning light cast on a bed
where two lay together—
the shining curve of flesh!—
they will forever be out of your reach
whose care is with the husks.
—MICHELE MURRAY, "DEATH POEM"

Reading
Now there are some things we all know, but we don't tak'm
out and look at'm very often. We all know that *something* is
eternal. And it ain't houses and it ain't names, and it ain't
earth, and it ain't even the stars. . . . Everybody knows in
their bones that something is eternal, and that *something*
has to do with human beings. All the greatest people ever
lived have been telling us that for five thousand years and
yet you'd be surprised how people are always losing hold
of it.
—THORNTON WILDER, *OUR TOWN*

Scripture
Martha and Mary sent word to Jesus from Bethany that
their brother, Lazarus, whom Jesus dearly loved was close
to death. Jesus said to his friends, "This illness is not to
end in death. It is for the glory of God and of his Son."
Now Jesus loved the two sisters and their brother, but nonetheless he stayed where he was another two days. Finally
he told his friends, "All right. Now we go back to Judea."
He said this, even though he knew he was under threat of
death himself if he came that near the high priests.
    When they arrived, he found Lazarus had already been
entombed four days. Typically, Martha met him on the road,
while Mary stayed home. "Lord," she said, controlling her
disappointment, "if you'd been here, my brother wouldn't
have died. But even now, I know whatever you ask, God

will give you." Jesus said quietly, "Your brother will rise." Martha's mouth pinched. "Yes. I know he will rise on the last day." Jesus put his hand on her shoulder. "Martha, *I* am resurrection and the life. Those who believe in me, even though they die, will live. Whoever lives believing in me will *never* die. Can you truly accept that?" Tears rolled down her cheeks, but she nodded. "Yes, Lord. I believe you are the Christ, the Son of God, the one who will rule the last day."

At the tomb, Jesus stood still, openly weeping, by the stone that covered the cave. "Take away the stone," he said. But Martha pushed forward. "Lord, no. He's been gone four days. The stench." But Jesus smiled at her. "Didn't you tell me you believed?" So they removed the stone, and Jesus cried out, "Lazarus! Come out!" Instantly, the dead man emerged from the shadows, still wrapped in his funeral cloths. Jesus said, "Unwrap him, and let him go."

—JOHN 11:3–7, 17, 20–27, 33–45

Closing
God, my Friend,
if we never comprehend death,
we can never comprehend resurrection
or value Christ's gift to us.
Amen.

✤ Evening

Presence
Great Friend,
what fear have I of death,
when my Brother has nullified death
    forever.

Grace
Abba, let me face whatever You plan without fears.

Psalm
Yes, all the things I once thought so important
I now see as wastes of time and futile desires
contrasted to the sublime privilege of knowing Christ.
I'm willing to slough them off as worthless trash
if only I can infuse my life into His.
All my sufferings merge me into His death,
and that union fuses my life into His resurrection.
I have yet to grasp that prize, but I strain toward it
as Christ reached out and strained to capture me.
—PHILIPPIANS 3:7–12

Hymn
Arise, my soul, arise!
Shake off thy guilty fears;
The bleeding Sacrifice
In my behalf appears.
Before the throne my surety stands;
My name is written on His hands.

The Father hears Him pray,
His dear anointed One;
He cannot turn away
The presence of His Son:
His Spirit answers to the blood,
And tells me that I am born of God.

My God is reconciled,
His pardoning voice I hear;
He owns me for His child,
I can no longer fear:
With confidence I now draw nigh,
And "Father, Abba, Father" cry.

—CHARLES WESLEY

Closing
Holy Friend,
my life is not a test
but a running start.
Amen.

Fifth Monday

✤ Morning

Presence
Great Friend,
when I am ready to jump to judgment,
make me get into the offender's shoes
   and walk in them awhile.

Grace
Abba, let me no longer set conditions on forgiveness.

Psalm
From now on, we judge no one by externals,
by human limitations, but only by the Spirit.
We once judged Jesus, earthbound, and we were wrong.
For anyone who is within Christ is in a *new* creation.
The old ways were justice; the new ways are mercy.
All this comes from God making peace with us
because of the amnesty Christ declared for sinners.
"Come one, come all! To unconditional forgiveness!"
Christ enfolds all in the world within Himself,
not holding our lifetime's faults against us.
And God missions each of us to cry, "Come home!"
—2 CORINTHIANS 5:16–19

Hymn
Is there a heart o'er-bound by sorrow?
Is there a life weighed down by care?
Come to the cross—each burden bearing,
All your anxiety—leave it there.
All your anxiety, all your care,
Bring to the mercy seat—leave it there;
Never a burden He cannot bear,
Never a friend like Jesus.

No other friend so keen to help you,
No other friend so quick to hear;
No other place to leave your burden,
No other one to hear your prayer.

Come then at once—delay no longer!
Heed His entreaty kind and sweet;
You need not fear a disappointment—
You shall find peace at the mercy seat.

Dedication

God, my Friend,
I offer You each moment of this day:
whatever comes—the unexpected challenges,
   diversions from my plans,
   the need-filled glance,
   the expectations and complaints,
   the being taken for granted,
   the slights and sleights-of-hand.
I'd be grateful if You could keep me aware of my pesky
      habits, like . . .
And, between us, perhaps we can enliven the spirits of
      those I live and work with, like . . .
Whatever else befalls,
   I trust we can cope with it,
     together.
Amen.

✢ Daytime

Presence

Great Friend,
sins of sexual weakness
don't seem to be as high on Your list of priorities
as I have been led to believe.

Grace

Abba, let my soul resonate with others as imperfect as I.

Psalm

In Jesus, the Son of God, we have our supreme high
      priest,
who has gone through it all but now resides in innermost
      heaven.
We must keep a firm grasp on our conviction He pleads
      for us.
Unlike other high priests, He has lived our reality,
shared exactly the same weaknesses we suffer,
yielded to every test we must face, except for sin.
Therefore, when we approach the throne of grace,
we approach One of our own who, despite His
      sinlessness,
has a greater fellow-feeling for sinners than we do.
—HEBREWS 4:14–16

Hymn

What if this present were the world's last night?
Mark in my heart, O soul, where thou dost dwell,
The picture of Christ crucified, and tell
Whether His countenance can thee affright.
Tears in His eyes quench the amazing light;
Blood fills his frowns, which from His pierced head fell;
And can that tongue adjudge thee unto hell,
Which pray'd forgiveness for His foes' fierce spite?
No, no; but as in my idolatry
I said to all my profane mistresses,
Beauty of pity, foulness only is
A sign of rigour; so I say to thee,
To wicked spirits are horrid shapes assign'd;
This beauteous form assures a piteous mind.
—JOHN DONNE, *HOLY SONNETS XIII*

Reading

Four times (at least) in the New Testament, Jesus deals one-on-one with sinners: the woman "known as a sinner in the town" (LK 7:36–50), the adulterous woman (JN 8:1–11), the Samaritan woman at the well (JN 4:1–26), and—at least by extension—the father of the prodigal son (LK 15:11–31). In not one case does Jesus make the sinner grovel. In not one case does he ask for specific sins and their numbers. In not one case does he give a retributory penance. In the first case, the woman doesn't say a word, merely weeps on his feet and dries them with her hair. But Jesus says, "Much is forgiven her because she has loved much." Jesus gives the adulterous woman the closest thing to a penance in telling her to avoid that sin in the future. The Samaritan woman says she has no husband, and Jesus says, "True enough. You've had five, and the one you live with now isn't your husband." He summarily drops that and goes on to talk about more important things, like eternal life. The prodigal's father runs to the boy, not the other way round, embraces the kid and kisses him *before* the boy's able to get out a single word of his apology! And he doesn't give him a penance; he gives him a party! If that's the way Jesus treated sinners, then it behooves us—no matter our rules—to treat them the same way.

—William O'Malley, *God: The Oldest Question*

Scripture

At daybreak Jesus came to the Temple again and sat down to teach the people who had come to listen to him. The officials pushed through, shoving ahead of them a disheveled woman, forcing her to stand directly in front of Jesus. "*Learned* Master," they smiled, "this wench was caught in the very act of adultery. Moses says such a woman should be stoned. And, uh, just what do *you*, from your *great* store of insight, have to say on this matter?" But Jesus leaned over and began drawing something in the dirt with his finger.

"*Learned* Master," they persisted, "your answer?" Jesus straightened up and nodded. "Yes. Whichever among you is sinless, let him hurl the first stone." Then he bent back down and continued drawing in the dust. The professional holy men looked momentarily taken aback at his boldness. They looked first sideways at the ground, then very cautiously under their brows, left and right. Then, gradually, they began to drift away one by one, beginning with the eldest. Finally, the last was gone, and Jesus was left alone with the woman, cowering in shame and fear in the middle of the empty courtyard. Jesus straightened up yet again and said, "Woman, where have they gone? Did no one dare condemn you?" She shrugged nervously. "No one, sir," she whispered." "Then neither do I condemn you," Jesus said. "Go now. And from now on avoid this sin, yes?"

—John 8:1–11

Closing
God, my Friend,
help me to share
the empathy of Your Son.
Amen.

✟ Evening

Presence
Great Friend,
thank You for the peace
that comes with Your forgiveness.

Grace
Abba, let me be a sign of forgiveness, too.

Psalm
Blessed be the Lord, the God of His People,
for He has visited us and set us free,

set the sign of salvation at the center of our lives.
This was the oath He swore to our father Abraham,
that He would grant us protection from the need to fear.
And you, child Jesus, will become the Prophet of the
        Most High,
for you will prepare the way for our sovereign God
and save His People through forgiveness of their sins
because of the never-ending love of God.
You light the way for those who live in darkness
and guide our steps through the shadows into peace.

—Luke 1:68–79

Hymn
Jesus, Refuge of the weary,
Blest Redeemer, whom we love,
Fountain in life's desert dreary,
Savior from the world above,
Oh, how oft Thine eyes, offended,
Gaze upon the sinner's fall!
Yet, upon the cross extended,
Thou didst bear the pain of all.

Do we pass that cross unheeding,
Breathing no repentant vow,
Though we see Thee wounded, bleeding,
See Thy thorn-encircled brow?
Yet Thy sinless death hath brought us
Life eternal, peace, and rest;
Only what Thy grace hath taught us
Calms the sinner's stormy breast.

Jesus, may our hearts be burning
With more fervent love for Thee!
May our eyes be ever turning
To Thy cross of agony
Till in glory, parted never

From the blessed Savior's side,
Graven in our hearts forever
Dwell the cross, the Crucified!

—GIROLAMO SAVONAROLA

Closing

Holy Friend,
the daylight eases into night,
but Your light never fails.
Amen.

Fifth Tuesday

✠ Morning

Presence
Great Friend,
everything that exists
draws its being from Your
unique "I AM."

Grace
Abba, let my confidence stand on Your presence within
me.

Psalm
The Lord spoke to Moses from within the fiery bush:
"You have forgotten the misery of your people, haven't
   you?
Well, I have not. I have come to rescue them.
I am sending an emissary to force the Pharaoh to free
   them."
The Lord's voice became very soft. "I'm sending . . . you."
Moses' heart—and jaw—plummeted. "What? *What?*
Sir, uh, who . . . who am *I* to challenge . . . Pharaoh?"
"You will not go alone," God said. "I will be with you."
Moses shifted from one bare foot to the other.
"Now, uh, look. Suppose I do, uh, go to the Pharaoh
and say, 'The God of our ancestors says you're to free us.'
They'll . . . they'll *howl* at me! 'What? Who is this . . .
   God?
Why, you fool, you don't even know His name!'"
The Lord thundered, "I AM! The Only God!
In My Name you will have all the power you need."
                                        —Exodus 3:7–13

Hymn

Flung to the heedless winds
Or on the waters cast,
The martyrs' ashes, watched,
Shall gathered be at last.
And from that scattered dust,
Around us and abroad,
Shall spring a plenteous seed
Of witnesses for God.

The Father hath received
Their latest living breath,
And vain is Satan's boast
Of victory in their death.
Still, still, though dead, they speak,
And, trumpet-tongued, proclaim
To many a wakening land
The one availing Name.

—MARTIN LUTHER

Dedication

God, my Friend,
I offer You each moment of this day:
whatever comes—the unexpected challenges,
   diversions from my plans,
   the need-filled glance,
   the expectations and complaints,
   the being taken for granted,
   the slights and sleights-of-hand.
I'd be grateful if You could keep me aware of my pesky
      habits, like . . .
And, between us, perhaps we can enliven the spirits of
      those I live and work with, like . . .
Whatever else befalls,
   I trust we can cope with it,
   together.
Amen.

✢ Daytime

Presence
Great Friend,
even the most unnerving challenges
carry within them a kernel of truth.

Grace
Abba, let my doubts be an invitation to seek better answers.

Psalm
You, my dear friends, must root yourselves in the
      foundation
of our sacred faith, relying on God's Holy Spirit.
Wrap yourselves in the undying love of God
and open your arms to the mercy of His life-giving
      Christ.
Be compassionate with those wavering, unsure, in doubt.
Be watchful for those who seem to be wandering off.
But challenge those whose souls are as soiled as their
      garments.

—JUDE 20–23

Hymn
Father hear the prayer we offer:
not for ease that prayer shall be,
But for strength that we may ever
Live our lives courageously.

Not for ever in green pastures
Do we ask our way to be;
But the steep and rugged pathway
May we tread, rejoicingly.

Not for ever by still waters
Would we idly rest and stay;

But would smite the living fountains
From the rocks along the way.

Be our strength in hours of weakness,
in our wanderings be our guide;
Through endeavour, failure, danger,
Father be Thou at our side.

Reading

O Lord, remember not only the men and women of good-will, but also those of ill-will. But do not only remember all the suffering they have inflicted on us, remember the fruits we bought thanks to this suffering, our comradeship, our loyalty, our humility, the courage, the generosity, the greatness of heart which has grown out of all this, and when they come to judgement, let all the fruits we have borne be their forgiveness.

—Sir Thomas More

Scripture

Jesus said to the people, "I'm going away. You can try to look for me, but if you don't believe I am who I claim to be, you will never know where to look—to your loss. Where I am going, you with your hardened hearts cannot come." So the religious officials puzzled over that. "What? Is he going to kill himself? Is that why he says he'll be out of our reach?" Jesus sighed. "Oh, you're so tied down to this world. I'm caught up in a world you simply refuse to allow! Yes, you will die in your stubborn blindness. You simply can't accept that I am who I say I am!" The leaders fumed. "All right, then. Just who *are* you?" Jesus let out a deep breath. "What I've been *telling* you from the very beginning! As truly as the judgments I've passed on you are true, ratified by the One who sent me and empowered me to speak for Him. That's the One you doubt—not me, but the One who sent me." They hadn't the slightest notion he was speaking of his Father. So Jesus went on, grimly: "When you have lifted up the Son of Man, then there might be a chance you will recognize that I am who I claim to be. What I say is what the Father taught me. He has never left me alone, and I will never cease to do what it pleases Him to ask of me."

—JOHN 8:21–30

Closing
God, my Friend,
help me discern
among so many conflicting certitudes.
Amen.

✢ Evening

Presence
Great Friend,
You speak in many voices,
    rarely clear,
    often cryptic,
    always without warning.

Grace
Abba, keep me attentive.

Psalm
Very late at night, while the nearly blind priest Eli slept,
the boy, Samuel, lay in the Temple where the Ark
of the Covenant gleamed under the sanctuary lamp.
A Voice called, "Samuel! Samuel!" The boy sprang
      awake.
"I'm here," he called and ran to old Eli's bed.
"Here I am, Master. You called me," he said.
The old priest muttered, "No child. Go back to sleep."
Three times the Voice called, and the boy obeyed.

Only then did the old man know Who had called the
      boy.
"Next time say, 'Speak, Lord. Your servant is listening.'"
                                        —1 SAMUEL 3:1–9

Hymn

O give me Samuel's ear,
The open ear, O Lord,
Alive and quick to hear
Each whisper of Thy Word,
Like him to answer at Thy call,
And to obey Thee first of all.

O give me Samuel's heart,
A lowly heart, that waits
Where in Thy house Thou art,
Or watches at Thy gates;
By day and night, a heart that still
Moves at the breathing of Thy will.

O give me Samuel's mind,
A sweet unmurm'ring faith,
Obedient and resigned
To Thee in life and death,
That I may read with child like eyes
Truths that are hidden from the wise.
                            —JAMES D. BURNS (1857)

Closing

Holy Friend,
teach me to be simple
without being a simpleton.
Amen.

Fifth Wednesday

✝ Morning

Presence
Great Friend,
before I begin today,
I must pull my self together.

Grace
Abba, let me keep—and share—my amazement that You've
chosen me.

Psalm
Because the Law is dead, I'm alive to a greater law,
where love has replaced the fear mere obedience
        implies.
I'm identified with Christ, crucified with Him but alive
        again!
The power, the energy, the soul in me is not "me" but
        Christ!
I need no confidence in myself but God's confidence in
        me.
I refuse to deny God's grace: Christ loved and died for
        me.
If a living friendship with God could come from keeping
        rules,
then Christ went through His death for no reason at all.
                                    —GALATIANS 2:19–23

Hymn
I shall gather myself into my self again,
I shall take my scattered selves and make them one.
I shall fuse them into a polished crystal ball
Where I can see the moon and the flashing sun.

I shall sit like a sibyl, hour after hour intent.
Watching the future come and the present go—
And the little shifting pictures of people rushing
In tiny self-importance to and fro.
—SARA TEASDALE, *THE CRYSTAL GAZER*

Dedication

God, my Friend,
I offer You each moment of this day:
whatever comes—the unexpected challenges,
   diversions from my plans,
   the need-filled glance,
   the expectations and complaints,
   the being taken for granted,
   the slights and sleights-of-hand.
I'd be grateful if You could keep me aware of my pesky
         habits, like . . .
And, between us, perhaps we can enliven the spirits of
         those I live and work with, like . . .
Whatever else befalls,
   I trust we can cope with it,
   together.
Amen.

✟ Daytime

Presence

Great Friend,
all the rule books have cracks and loopholes
that love seals up.

Grace

Abba, remind me that "neighbor" has no conditions or exceptions.

Psalm

Blame can never fall on those in Christ Jesus;
the law of love frees us from the Law of guilt.

Because of human weakness for weaseling, the Law
 failed.
But in offering humanity in sacrifice Christ cleansed it.
Those led by instincts are as enslaved as beasts;
Those who follow the Spirit are free of fear and death,
for the animal in us ceases to live when we die.
But the Spirit has made her home within you.
Then the Spirit of Him who raised Christ from the
 dead
will give eternal life even now within your mortal bodies.
If by the Spirit you put to death the habits
arising from your lower self, you will have life!
—Romans 8:1–13

Hymn

Thou shalt have one God only; who
Would be at the expense of two?
No graven images may be
Worshiped, except the currency:
Swear not at all; for, for thy curse
Thine enemy is none the worse:
At church on Sunday to attend
Will serve to keep the world thy friend:
Honour thy parents; that is, all
From whom advancement may befall:
Thou shalt not kill; but need'st not strive
Officiously to keep alive:
Do not adultery commit;
Advantage rarely comes of it:
Thou shalt not steal; an empty feat,
When it's so lucrative to cheat:
Bear not false witness; let the lie
Have time on its own wings to fly:
Thou shalt not covet, but tradition
Approves all forms of competition.
—Arthur Hugh Clough, *The Last Decalogue*

Reading

Is there a union scale for the corporal works of mercy and rescue? Miles to the contrary, money is the last come-on by which a Damien is lured to the lepers of Molokai, or a Martin de Porres to the slums of Lima, or a Dorothy Day to the Bowery. Something else induced them to get away and serve the wounded—a bigness of spirit which insists that wanton man-made cruelty is eased best by getting into the ditch with the victims.

—COLMAN MCCARTHY, *INNER COMPANIONS*

Scripture

In order to put Jesus to the test, a Temple lawyer asked, "Sir, what must I do to live a life that fulfills God's will?" Jesus answered simply, "You know the Law. What does it say?" The man huffed, "Love God with all your heart and your neighbor as yourself." Jesus said, "Fine. Now do it." But the man, miffed that he had been so easily tripped up, asked, "And who *is* my neighbor?" Instead of answering directly, Jesus told a story. "Once upon a time a man was going from Jerusalem to Jericho and was attacked by bandits, who beat him, stripped him, and ran off, leaving him half-dead. Now a worthy priest happened by, caught sight of the man, and distracted himself with the scenery on the other side of the road. Then a layman who served the Temple, like yourself, came by and found other things to occupy his interest. Then a heretic Samaritan came upon the victim and was moved with compassion. He cleaned and bandaged his wounds, then put him on his own mount and took him to an inn to be cared for. Next day, he gave money to the innkeeper to look after the man and promised he'd make good any further expenses on his way back. Now, which of these three do you think proved to be a neighbor to the beaten man?" The lawyer blushed and turned away, grunting, "The . . . the one who showed pity." Jesus smiled. "Fine again. Now do it."

—LUKE 10:25–37

Closing
God, my Friend,
bring them on!
I'll try my best.
Amen.

✟ Evening

Presence
Great Friend,
at this point in the Lenten season,
it seems as if
it will never end.

Grace
Abba, lead me. I'm ready to follow.

Psalm 143
Lord, if you focus on trifles, no one human stands a
          chance.
But I do at times grow weary, unsure of my worth,
wary of arrogance, vanity, holier-than-thou.
But I place my trust in You and not myself.
Show me the road I must travel with an easy heart.
May Your generous Spirit lead me, unfretful, trusting.
Let me rejoice that You've made me Your servant,
not a nobody but a chosen peer of Your Realm.

Hymn
Lead, Kindly Light, amid the encircling gloom,
Lead Thou me on!
The night is dark, and I am far from home—
Lead Thou me on!
Keep Thou my feet; I do not ask to see
The distant scene,—one step enough for me.
I was not ever thus, nor pray'd that Thou

Should'st lead me on.
I loved to choose and see my path; but now
Lead Thou me on!
I loved the garish day, and, spite of fears,
Pride ruled my will: remember not past years.

So long Thy power hath blest me, sure it still
Will lead me on,
O'er moor and fen, o'er crag and torrent, till
The night is gone;
And with the morn those angel faces smile
Which I have loved long since, and lost awhile.

—JOHN HENRY CARDINAL NEWMAN

Closing

Holy Friend,
I'll come back tomorrow
with greater verve.
Promise.
Amen.

Fifth Thursday

✿ Morning

Presence
Great Friend,
even when Your reasons escape me,
I truly believe You have them.

Grace
Abba, let me show my gratitude by being gracious.

Psalm 105
Tirelessly seek the strength of the Lord's presence.
Remember His wonders since He ignited the first star!
The God who spoke to Abraham, Isaac, and Jacob
is with divine humility eager to be with you.
The promises He made to thousands of generations
He yearns to see come to fulfillment in you.
He sits at the door of our tent as He did with the
        patriarchs.
He summons you from slavery as He did His People in
        Egypt.
He calls you to forsake your shyness as He did the
        prophets.
He has plans for you, today and all of your days.

Hymn
Still, still with Thee, when purple morning breaketh,
When the bird waketh and the shadows flee;
Fairer than morning, lovelier than daylight,
Dawns the sweet consciousness I am with Thee.
Alone with Thee, amid the mystic shadows,
The solemn hush of nature newly born;

Alone with Thee in breathless adoration,
In the calm dew and freshness of the morn.
Still, still to Thee, as to each new-born morning,
A fresh and solemn splendor still is giv'n,
So does this blessed consciousness awaking,
Breathe each day nearness unto Thee and heav'n.
So shall it be at last in that bright morning,
When the soul waketh, and life's shadows flee;
O in that hour, fairer than daylight dawning,
Shall rise the glorious thought I am with Thee.
—HARRIET BEECHER STOWE

Dedication

God, my Friend,
I offer You each moment of this day:
whatever comes—the unexpected challenges,
   diversions from my plans,
   the need-filled glance,
   the expectations and complaints,
   the being taken for granted,
   the slights and sleights-of-hand.
I'd be grateful if You could keep me aware of my pesky
      habits, like . . .
And, between us, perhaps we can enliven the spirits of
      those I live and work with, like . . .
Whatever else befalls,
   I trust we can cope with it,
   together.
Amen.

✷ Daytime

Presence

Great Friend,
how arrogant of us
   to believe things would be so much better
if You only knew as much as we do.

Grace

Abba, let my mind be humble enough to listen to my soul.

Psalm

"Accept this in order to be at peace," says the Lord.
"My thoughts are not your thoughts, nor your ways My
    ways.
As distant as the farthest star are My ways above
    yours
and My thoughts as inaccessible to your thoughts.
But just as the rain and snow do not fall from the sky
without fulfilling My will—to water, to make fertile, to
    feed,
so it is with the Word that comes from within Me.
He will not return to Me with His promise fruitless.
He serves at My pleasure and will do what I sent Him to
    do."

—Isaiah 55:8–11

Hymn

O World, thou choosest not the better part!
It is not wisdom to be only wise,
And on the inward vision close the eyes,
But it is wisdom to believe the heart.
Columbus found a world, and had no chart,
Save one that faith deciphered in the skies;
To trust the soul's invincible surmise
Was all his science and his only art.
Our knowledge is a torch of smoky pine
That lights the pathway but one step ahead
Across a void of mystery and dread.
Bid, then, the tender light of faith to shine
By which alone the mortal heart is led
Unto the thinking of the thoughts divine.

—George Santayana

Reading

Sir James Jeans, British astronomer and physicist, suggested that the universe was beginning to look more like a great thought than a great machine. Humanists seized on the expression, but it was hardly news. We knew, looking around, that a thought branches and leafs, a tree comes to a conclusion. But the question of who is thinking the thought is more fruitful than the question of who made the machine, for a machinist can of course wipe his hands and leave, and his simple machine still hums; but if the thinker's attention strays for a minute, his simplest thought ceases altogether. And, as I have stressed, the place where we so incontrovertibly find ourselves, whether thought or machine, is at least not in any way simple.

—ANNIE DILLARD, *PILGRIM AT TINKER CREEK*

Scripture

Jesus asked his disciples, "Who do people think I am?" They stumbled and mumbled. "Uh, some say the Baptist, some say Elijah or Jeremiah or one of the other prophets come back again." "And you?" Jesus asked. "Who do you think I really am?" With typical forthrightness, Peter said, "You are the Christ. The Son of the living God." Jesus smiled. "Ah, Simon, son of Jonah, you are a man gifted by God. You didn't come to that by poring through texts or listening to others' ideas. My Father in heaven implanted that understanding in your heart. From now on, I tell you, you are Peter, the bedrock on whom I'll build the new People of God. You will hold the keys of that Kingdom. Whatever decisions you make in the Kingdom here will be ratified in the Kingdom in heaven, and the powers of darkness will never overcome it." Then he gave strict orders that for the time this must be kept secret.

From then on, Jesus began to make it clear to his people that he was destined to go up to Jerusalem, suffer at the hands of the religious leaders, and be killed. But he would rise on the third day. But Peter pulled him aside. "God help us, Lord! This must *not* happen. Not to *you*!" Jesus held his temper, but he growled, "Get out of my way, you devil! I thought you *understood*! But you think just like the rest. What the human mind refuses to accept is not unthinkable to God!"

—MATTHEW 16:13–23

Closing
God, my Friend,
You submit to our scrutiny,
but not to conquest.
Amen.

✢ Evening

Presence
Great Friend,
I will go gently
into Your good night.

Grace
Abba, let the way I live reveal my belief.

Psalm
Clues to the Spirit's presence within you should be
      obvious.
Mull them over, one by one, and reveal them:
unselfish love, exuberant joy, serenity,
patience, kindness, perseverance, trustfulness,
conviction of the basic goodness of all things and people,
gentleness in judgment and easy self-control.
No law can generate those, nor can it quell them.
For those who belong to Christ, all need for dominance
or slavish conformity have been crucified with Him.

We are not conceited or provocative or envious of one
   another.
The Spirit within us should be manifest in the way we live.
—GALATIANS 5:22–26

Hymn
Joyous light of heavenly glory,
   loving glow of God's own face,
You who sing creation's story,
   shine on every land and race.
Now the evening falls around us,
   we shall raise our songs to you,
God of daybreak, God of shadows,
   come and light our hearts anew.
In the stars that grace the darkness,
   the blazing sun of dawn,
In the light of peace and wisdom,
   we can hear your quiet song.
Love that fills the night with wonder,
   love that warms the weary soul.
Love that bursts all chains asunder,
   set us free and make us whole.
You who made the heaven's splendor,
   every dancing star of night,
Make us shine with gentle justice,
   let us each reflect your light.
Mighty God of all creation,
   gentle Christ who lights our way,
Loving Spirit of salvation,
   lead us on to endless day

Closing
Holy Friend,
I will try to make my life
a gift of thanksgiving.
Amen.

Fifth Friday

✛ Morning

Presence
Great Friend,
without You
everyone and everything
is spinning, slowly, slowly
　　toward annihilation.

Grace
Abba, remind me always: It's either You or . . . nothing.

Psalm 53
Fools have said in their hearts, "There is no God."
Their arguments are slithery as snakes, all self-serving.
God ponders us from heaven, wondering if
anyone since Adam has learned to think honestly.
Don't they realize "I" is the narrowest of words and
　　　　worlds?
They foul themselves when they poison rivers and skies.
Are they aware their profits devour the human soul?
They need no hell. They embody it in themselves.
Their self-absorption devours them from within,
and slowly there will be nothing left of them but a
　　　　whimper.

Hymn
"There is no God," the wicked saith,
　　"And truly it's a blessing,
For what He might have done with us
　　It's better only guessing." . . .

Some others, also, to themselves,
    Who scarce so much as doubt it,
Think there is none, when they are well,
    And do not think about it.
But country folks who live beneath
    The shadow of the steeple;
The parson and the parson's wife,
    And mostly married people;
Youths green and happy in first love,
    So thankful for illusion;
And men caught out in what the world
    Calls guilt, in first confusion;
And almost everyone when age,
    Disease, or sorrows strike him,
Inclines to think there is a God,
    Or something very like Him.

                   —ARTHUR HUGH CLOUGH

Dedication

God, my Friend,
I offer You each moment of this day:
whatever comes—the unexpected challenges,
    diversions from my plans,
    the need-filled glance,
    the expectations and complaints,
    the being taken for granted,
    the slights and sleights-of-hand.
I'd be grateful if You could keep me aware of my pesky
        habits, like . . .
And, between us, perhaps we can enliven the spirits of
        those I live and work with, like . . .
Whatever else befalls,
    I trust we can cope with it,
    together.
Amen.

✠ Daytime

Presence
Great Friend,
before Your Son became one of us,
You comprehended all that "human" means.
Now, you *know*.

Grace
Abba, remind me that nothing human is alien to You.

Psalm
Make your own mind the mind of Christ Jesus.
From before the beginning, He was equal to God,
but He didn't cling to the powers that reside in God.
Instead, He gave it all up—emptied Himself—
in order to become in every way as humans are.
He lived a selfless, obedient life—and death,
not just death, but excruciating death on a cross.
Because of that, God raised Him back up
and returned to Him the divine name and status.
Thus, all beings—in heaven, on earth, and in hell—
should bow in worship before the name of Jesus
and every voice confess Jesus Christ is Lord
to the eternal glory of our God and Father.

—PHILIPPIANS 2:6–11

Hymn
Crown Him with many crowns,
The Lamb upon His throne;
Hark! how the heav'nly anthem drowns
All music but its own!
Awake, my soul, and sing
Of Him who died for thee,
And hail Him as thy matchless King
Through all eternity.

Crown Him the Virgin's Son,
The God Incarnate born,
Whose arm those crimson trophies won
Which now His brow adorn:
Fruit of the mystic Tree,
As of that Tree the Stem;
The Root whence flows Thy mercy free,
The Babe of Bethlehem.

Crown Him the Lord of years,
The Potentate of time.
Creator of the rolling spheres,
Ineffable sublime.
All hail, Redeemer, hail!
For Thou hast died for me;
Thy praise shall never, never fail
Throughout eternity.

—MATTHEW BRIDGES

Reading

There is no halfway house and there is no parallel in other religions. If you had gone to Buddha and said "Are you the son of Bramah?" he would have said "My son, you are still in the veil of illusion." If you had gone to Socrates and asked, "Are you Zeus?" he would have laughed at you. If you had gone to Mohammed and asked "Are you Allah?" he would first have rent his clothes and then cut your head off. If you had asked Confucius "Are you heaven?" I think he would probably have replied, "Remarks which are not in accordance with nature are in bad taste." The idea of a great moral teacher saying what Christ said is out of the question. In my opinion, the only person who can say that sort of thing is either God or a complete lunatic suffering from that form of delusion which undermines the whole mind of man. If you think you are a poached egg, when you are not looking for a piece of toast to suit you, you may

be sane, but if you think you are God, there is no chance
for you. We may note in passing that He was never re-
garded as a mere moral teacher. He did not produce that
effect on any of the people who actually met Him. He pro-
duced mainly three effects—Hatred—Terror—Adoration.
There was no trace of people expressing mild approval.

—C. S. LEWIS, "WHAT ARE WE TO MAKE OF JESUS CHRIST?"

Scripture

When Jesus dared to say, "The Father and I are one," the
pious Jews pawed around to find rocks to stone him. So Jesus
said, "Which of the good works I've done through the power
of my Father are you stoning me for?" They could hardly
contain their rage: "We're not stoning you for any good work!
You've *blasphemed*! Oh, we understand you *now*! You're only
a *man*! And you dare to claim to be . . . *God*?" Jesus held up
his hands. "Wait. Doesn't it say in our psalms [82:6]: 'You
are gods'? If it uses the word 'gods' of those to whom the
word of God is addressed—and the scriptures don't lie—
then why do you cry, 'Blasphemy!' at the unique messenger
sent by God when I say, 'I am the Son of God'? If I'm not
doing my Father's work, then reject me. But if I *am* doing
God's work, then you're rejecting the evidence you have
right before your eyes! At the very least you can't deny the
work I've been doing. It is the work of *God*. Because the
Father is in me, and I am in the Father." They tried to grab
him once again, but he eluded their clutches.

—JOHN 10:31–39

Closing

God, my Friend,
there are so many good-hearted people
who don't realize how barren and absurd life is
unless Someone
   has a reason for it all.
Amen.

✟ Evening

Presence
Great Friend,
I'm like someone blind
   in a world so alive
   with abundance of light and life.

Grace
Abba, help me reach beyond my senses.

Psalm 114
The seas rucked up their backs and fled at the sight.
Mountains skipped like rams, and hills leaped high in
      delight.
Great waters, what awesome power do you fear to face?
You mountains and hills, why do you frolic with glee?
Tremble, earth, at the coming of the Source of All!
The Wellspring of Life who turned rock into pools
and made flint rise up and cascade in fiery fountains.
His power surges and pulses within all-that-is!

Hymn
No lily-muffled hum of a summer-bee,
But finds some coupling with the spinning stars;
No pebble at your foot, but proves a sphere;
No chaffinch, but implies the cherubim:
And—glancing on my own thin, veined wrist—
In such a little tremour of the blood
The whole strong clamour of a vehement soul
Doth utter itself distinct. Earth's crammed with heaven,
And every common bush afire with God:
But only he who sees, takes off his shoes,
The rest sit round it, and pluck blackberries,
          —ELIZABETH BARRETT BROWNING, *AURORA LEIGH*

Closing

Holy Friend,
I go to my rest
    surrounded with such splendor.
Amen.

Fifth Saturday

✠ Morning

Presence
Great Friend,
if I can feel secure in You,
I can feel secure in myself.

Grace
Abba, keep my chin stuck out, unafraid of being socked.

Psalm
Listen, People of God, dispersed all over the world!
He who allowed you to scatter away from Him
is calling you back, like a shepherd whistling to his flock.
He will go ransom for you, redeeming you from
        enslavements.
Come home, shouting for joy! You will grieve no more!
You girls and boys—and old people, too—will dance!
Mourning and sorrow will be reborn into joy!
                                    —Jeremiah 31:1–13

Hymn
Where the mind is without fear and the head is held high
Where knowledge is free
Where the world has not been broken up into fragments
By narrow domestic walls
Where words come out from the depth of truth
Where tireless striving stretches its arms towards
        perfection
Where the clear stream of reason has not lost its way
Into the dreary desert sand of dead habit
Where the mind is led forward by thee

Into ever-widening thought and action
Into that heaven of freedom, my Father, let my country
    awake.

                                        —RABINDRANATH TAGORE

Dedication

God, my Friend,
I offer You each moment of this day:
whatever comes—the unexpected challenges,
    diversions from my plans,
    the need-filled glance,
    the expectations and complaints,
    the being taken for granted,
    the slights and sleights-of-hand.
I'd be grateful if You could keep me aware of my pesky
    habits, like . . .
And, between us, perhaps we can enliven the spirits of
    those I live and work with, like . . .
Whatever else befalls,
    I trust we can cope with it,
    together.
Amen.

✠ Daytime

Presence

Great Friend,
to quote, if I may, Francis Albert Sinatra,
"You show me a man without enemies,
    and I'll show you a coward."

Grace

Abba, they misjudged Your son. Don't let me expect anything more.

Psalm 56
Take pity on me, O God, they haunt my footsteps.
When I'm tempted to fear, I put my trust in You.
What merely human threat can surmount Your
    protection?
Still, they carp at my words, trying to trip me up,
sneer at my confidence in You as my own arrogance.
This I know for certain: God is on my side.
You've braced me up when I feared I was ready to fall.
But I walk in the presence of God in the light of the
    living!

Hymn
Death stands above me, whispering low
I know not what into my ear:
Of his strange language all I know
Is, there is not a word of fear.
           —WALTER SAVAGE LANDOR

Reading
The people who hanged Christ never, to do them justice, accused him of being a bore—on the contrary; they thought him too dynamic to be safe. It has been left for later generations to muffle up that shattering personality and surround him with an atmosphere of tedium. We have very efficiently pared the claws of the Lion of Judah, certified him "meek and mild," and recommended him as a fitting household pet for pale curates and pious old ladies.

To those who knew him, however, he in no way suggested a milk-and-water person; they objected to him as a dangerous firebrand. True, he was tender to the unfortunate, patient with honest inquirers and humble before Heaven; but he insulted respectable clergymen by calling them hypocrites; he referred to King Herod as "that fox"; he went to parties in disreputable company and was looked upon as a "gluttonous man and a wine-bibber, friend of publicans and sinners"; he assaulted indignant tradesmen and threw them and their belongings out of the Temple; he drove a coach-and-horses through a number of sacrosanct and hoary regulations; he cured diseases by any means that came handy, with a shocking casualness in the matter of other people's pigs and property; he showed no proper deference for wealth or social position; when confronted with neat dialectical traps, he displayed a paradoxical humor that affronted serious-minded people, and he retorted by asking disagreeably searching questions that could not be answered by rule of thumb. He was emphatically not a dull man in his human lifetime, and if he was God, there can be nothing dull about God either. But he had "a daily beauty in his life that made us ugly," and officialdom felt that the established order of things would be more secure without him. So they did away with God in the name of peace and quietness.

—Dorothy Sayers, "The Greatest Drama"

Scripture

As a result of Lazarus's return from the dead, many believed in Jesus. But some crept off to tell the Pharisees what Jesus had done. The religious leaders and the Pharisees called an emergency meeting. "Here is this intruder, pulling off these magic tricks! And what are we *doing* about it? If we let him go on, the whole stinking rabble will rally behind him, and the Romans will get nervous. They'll take away the *Temple*! They'll crush what little independence they've left us!" One of them, Caiaphas, quite sure of himself as high priest for the year, looked at them with disdain. "Really. None of you has grasped the situation at all! Can't you see all this is to our advantage? Cut off the head, and our worries are over! Take the long view, brothers. Which is better? That one man die, or that the whole nation perish?" In his self-importance, he believed he was prophesying that Jesus would die for the Jewish nation, when actually he would

die so that all the world's scattered nations could be gathered into one flock. But from that day on, they began to
plot specific tactics to get him killed. Jesus no longer went
openly among them but left with his disciples for Ephraim,
near the desert.

—JOHN 11:45–54

Closing
God, my Friend,
shore up my confidence,
which is less than perfect.
Amen.

✢ Evening

Presence
Great Friend,
my task is to confirm in all I meet
the dignity each has
simply by being made in Your image.

Grace
Abba, let me rest secure each day, knowing I tried my best.

Psalm 15
Lord God, who can find a home within Your tent?
You welcome all who try to live uprightly,
to speak the truth, kindly, right from the heart,
yet know when it's wise to set a guard on their tongues,
who say yes when they mean yes and no when they mean
        no.
Those find rest with You who'd never wrong a comrade
nor damage the reputation of a neighbor,
whose word alone needs no other collateral.
Their self-interest never outweighs the interests of
        others.

Nothing could persuade them to harm the innocent or
        lie.
No one who lives that way will ever be forsaken.

Hymn
The day thou gavest, Lord, is ended,
The darkness falls at thy behest;
To thee our morning hymns ascended,
Thy praise shall sanctify our rest.

We thank thee that thy Church unsleeping,
While earth rolls onward into light,
Through all the world her watch is keeping,
And rests not now by day or night.

As o'er each continent and island
The dawn leads on another day,
The voice of prayer is never silent,
Nor dies the strain of praise away.

—JOHN ELLERTON (1870)

Closing
Holy Friend,
I confess my belief that,
    unlike Yourself,
the world can get along
    without me
    for a while.
Amen.

Palm Sunday

✠ Morning

Presence
Great Friend,
to echo Thomas, the doubt-filled,
"All right, then.
Let's go up to the city
   and die with Him."

Grace
Abba, help me remember this week's events are still going
on.

Psalm
The Lord God has given me a prophet's tongue
so I know how to speak words of comfort to the weary.
Morning after morning, He wakens my ears, alert
to catch every nuance of His wishes for me.
I have not resisted, nor have I turned away.
I offered my back without protest to those who lashed
      me,
stood firm when they mocked me and plucked my beard.
I did not shield my face from their fists and spittle.
They can batter my flesh but never possess my soul.
The Lord is my help. I can never be truly disgraced.
I have set my face like flint. They cannot shame me.
          —Isaiah 50:4–7

Hymn
Wide fields of corn along the valleys spread;
The rain and dews mature the swelling vine;
I see the Lord is multiplying bread;

I see Him turning water into wine;
I see Him working all the works divine
He wrought when Salemward His steps were led;
The selfsame miracles around Him shine;
He feeds the famished; He revives the dead;
He pours the flood of light on darkened eyes;
He chases tears, diseases, fiends away;
His throne is raised upon these western skies;
His footstool is the pave whereon we pray.
Ah, tell me not of Christ in Paradise,
For He is all around us here to-day.
　　　　　—JOHN CHARLES EARLE, *"LO, I AM WITH YOU ALWAYS"*

Dedication
God, my Friend,
I offer You each moment of this day:
whatever comes—the unexpected challenges,
　　diversions from my plans,
　　the need-filled glance,
　　the expectations and complaints,
　　the being taken for granted,
　　the slights and sleights-of-hand.
I'd be grateful if You could keep me aware of my pesky
　　　　habits, like . . .
And, between us, perhaps we can enliven the spirits of
　　　　those I live and work with, like . . .
Whatever else befalls,
　　I trust we can cope with it,
　　together.
Amen.

✢ Daytime

Presence
Great Friend,
today is a bitter (and disregarded) lesson

for all those
> who base their sense of value
> on the approval of the crowds.

Grace
Abba, remind me always that true worth is always invisible.

Psalm
Aha! Rejoice, heart and soul, daughter of Zion!
Sing out your lungs with joy, daughter Jerusalem!
Your king is approaching! He's coming! He's *coming!*
Within him he carries the power to set all things right.
But he comes humbly, riding on a donkey's foal.
He will banish horse chariots and all the weapons of war.
He will proclaim a realm of peace from sea to sea,
from wherever he is to the limits of the earth.
—ZECHARIAH 9:9–10

Hymn
When forests walked and fishes flew
And figs grew upon thorn,
Some moment when the moon was blood,
Then, surely, I was born.

With monstrous head and sickening bray
And ears like errant wings—
The devil's walking parody
Of all four-footed things:

The battered outlaw of the earth
Of ancient crooked will;
Scourge, beat, deride me—I am dumb—
I keep my secret still.

Fools! For I also had my hour—
One far fierce hour and sweet:

There was a shout around my head
And palms about my feet.
—G. K. CHESTERTON, THE DONKEY

Reading

In her play, "The Man Born to Be King," Dorothy Sayers provides an intriguing insight into the motivation of the apostle Judas for perpetrating the most heinous betrayal in all history. In her portrayal, Judas had been a Zealot assassin, fiercely dedicated to ousting the Romans by force. (One root of his tag-name, "Iscariot," is *sicarius*, "dagger-man.") But Judas had been genuinely, profoundly converted from violence, from a political goal to a spiritual one—like the soldier Robert DeNiro played in "The Mission." For him, Palm Sunday came as a heart-stopping shock: Here was Jesus, the humble man of peace, with no pretensions to political power whatever, smilingly submitting to what might be compared to the screaming adulation at a modern nominating convention. Jesus—Judas's hero and ideal—had sold out! He'd been seduced by the trappings of power and the adoring crowds! Thus, in order to *save* Jesus from what Judas misread as Jesus' own weakness, Judas agreed to betray him. If Sayers is right, Judas's horrific treachery was a misguided act of love for a man he truly idolized.

Scripture

When Jesus and his friends drew near Jerusalem, near Bethphage and Bethany at the Mount of Olives, he sent two men ahead. "Go into that village over there, and you'll find a donkey colt no one has ever ridden, tethered right at the first house. Untie it and bring it here. If anyone asks what you're doing, say, 'The Master needs to borrow it, but he'll send it back right away.'" So they went and found the young donkey and untied it. Some of the neighbors called out, "What do you think you're doing there?" They explained as Jesus told them to, and the people seemed satisfied. They brought the colt to Jesus and laid their cloaks on it. Jesus climbed onto the little colt, and as they proceeded into the city, bystanders spread their own cloaks on the roadway, while others scattered leafy branches they'd cut in the fields. A crowd spread out ahead of him and ran jubilantly behind, crying out, "Hosanna! Blessed is he who comes in the name of the Lord! The Kingdom of David, our father, is ready to begin! Hosanna in the highest!"

—MARK 11:1–10

Closing
God, my Friend,
Your idea of importance
is so much different from ours.
Amen.

✦ Evening

Presence
Great Friend,
what Jesus did on this day
seems so unwise.
Or at least so . . . imprudent.

Grace
Abba, make me less cautious.

Psalm 83
O God, do not stay silent and unmoved!
Your enemies are laying plans against what You cherish.
If You wish, You can puff them away like thistledown,
like the empty husks they are, at the mercy of the wind!
You could wipe them out like a fire in a forest!
Instead, You stand aloof, while they take what is Your
       own.

Hymn

Lord, I have knelt and tried to pray to-night,
But Thy love came upon me like a sleep,
And all desire died out; upon the deep
Of Thy mere love I lay, each thought in light
Dissolving like the sunset clouds, at rest
Each tremulous wish, and my strength weakness, sweet
As a sick boy with soon o'erwearied feet
Finds, yielding him unto his mother's breast
To weep for weakness there. I could not pray,
But with closed eyes I felt Thy bosom's love
Beating toward mine, and then I would not move
Till of itself the joy should pass away;
At last my heart found voice,—"Take me, O Lord,
And do with me according to Thy word."
—EDWARD DOWDEN (D. 1913), "COMMUNION"

Closing

Holy Friend,
give me what Your Son had
    so unreservedly:
a willingness to be used.
Amen.

Monday of Holy Week

✟ Morning

Presence
Great Friend,
Your Son promised us *unconditional* forgiveness.
Help me answer
why I keep wanting to apologize.

Grace
Abba, keep open the connection between my heart and my
hands.

Psalm
Who's fooled, my friends, when some claim to have faith
but have never done a kind act in their lives?
If someone is standing in tatters begging for food,
and you say, "Ah! You have a nice day, d'ya hear?
I sure hope you can find better clothes than that,
and you really ought to put on some weight"—
but keep your wallets safe in pocket or purse,
what on God's green earth is the good of that?
That's what faith without action is: swamp gas.
—James 2:14–17

Hymn
For Mercy has a human heart,
Pity a human face,
And Love, the human form divine,
And Peace, the human dress.
Then every man, of every clime,
That prays in his distress,

Prays to the human form divine,
Love, Mercy, Pity, Peace.
And all must love the human form,
In heathen, Turk, or Jew;
Where Mercy, Love, and Pity dwell
There God is dwelling too.

—WILLIAM BLAKE, THE DIVINE IMAGE

Dedication

God, my Friend,
I offer You each moment of this day:
whatever comes—the unexpected challenges,
    diversions from my plans,
    the need-filled glance,
    the expectations and complaints,
    the being taken for granted,
    the slights and sleights-of-hand.
I'd be grateful if You could keep me aware of my pesky
        habits, like . . .
And, between us, perhaps we can enliven the spirits of
        those I live and work with, like . . .
Whatever else befalls,
    I trust we can cope with it,
    together.
Amen.

✢ Daytime

Presence

Great Friend,
You're so spendthrift with Your gifts.

Grace

Abba, help me share whatever I have and am.

Psalm

"Here is My servant, whom I stand behind,
My chosen one in whom My soul delights.
I've sent My Spirit upon him to act in judgment.
He will speak calmly, judiciously, honestly.
His heart will go out to the weak and stumbling.
He will not falter or back down until his task is done.
It is I who speak—the One who spread out the heavens,
who shaped the earth and infused it with teeming life,
who breathed the souls into the people who walk on it.
I have grasped you by the hand and made covenant with you,
to unseal blind eyes and shatter the prisoners' shackles,
to call forth all who cower in darkness into the light."
—Isaiah 42:1–7

Hymn

All are but parts of one stupendous whole,
Whose body Nature is, and God the soul;
That, changed through all, and yet in all the same,
Great in the earth, as in th' ethereal frame,
Warms in the sun, refreshes in the breeze,
Glows in the stars, and blossoms in the trees,
Lives through all life, extends through all extent,
Spreads undivided, operates unspent:
Breathes in our soul, informs our mortal part;
As full, as perfect, in a hair as heart;
As full, as perfect, in vile man that mourns,
As the rapt Seraphim, that sings and burns:
To him no high, no low, no great, no small—
He fills, he bounds, connects, and equals all. . . .
All nature is but art, unknown to thee:
All chance, direction, which thou canst not see:
All discord, harmony not understood;
All partial evil, universal good.
—Alexander Pope, *An Essay on Man*

Reading
The way in which a man accepts his fate and all the suffering it entails, the way in which he takes up his cross, gives him ample opportunity—even under the most difficult circumstances—to add a deeper meaning to his life. It may remain brave, dignified, and unselfish. Or in the bitter fight for self-preservation he may forget his human dignity and become no more than an animal. Here lies the chance for a man either to make use of or to forego the opportunities of attaining the moral values that a difficult situation may afford him. And this decides whether he is worthy of his sufferings or not.

—Viktor Frankl, *Man's Search for Meaning*

Scripture
Six days before Passover, Jesus visited Bethany for a dinner given for him by Lazarus, whom he had raised from the dead. Martha, his sister, waited on them. But as they reclined at table, Mary, the other sister, pushed through the guests and knelt at Jesus' feet. From a jar she poured a great gush of expensive aromatic oils on Jesus' feet and wiped them with her unbound hair. The heady fragrance filled the entire house. But Judas Iscariot (the one who would betray him) snapped, "This is disgraceful! That oil could have been sold for three hundred silver pieces! And given to the poor." (They wondered later if his concern was less for the poor than for the common purse he had charge of and, some thought, dipped into.) But Jesus shook his head. "Leave her alone. The rest she can save. For my burial. The poor will always be with you, but the time you have with me grows shorter every hour."

—John 12:1–8

Closing
God, my Friend,
even if others misuse the gifts I give,

I have not been a mean-spirited giver.
Amen.

♀ Evening

Presence
Great Friend,
so often "the wrath of God"
is the love of God,
assessed by a fool.

Grace
Abba, help me steadily build my patience and trust.

Psalm 35
Unprovoked, they laid a trap to capture me.
False witnesses came forward to accuse me.
They cross-examine me, repay my kindness with cruelty.
But when they were ill, I ministered to their pain,
I prayed for them and spent myself like a brother.
But when I stumble, they gather and giggle with glee.
Lord, You've seen it all, then why be silent?

Hymn
I missed him when the sun began to bend;
I found him not when I had lost his rim;
With many tears I went in search of him,
Climbing high mountains which did still ascend,
And gave me echoes when I called my friend;
Through cities vast and charnel-houses grim,
And high cathedrals where the light was dim,
Through books and arts and works without an end,
But found him not—the friend whom I had lost.
And yet I found him—as I found the lark,
A sound in fields I heard but could not mark;

I found him nearest when I missed him most;
I found him in my heart, a life in frost,
A light I knew not till my soul was dark.
—GEORGE MACDONALD, *LOST AND FOUND*

Closing
Holy Friend,
I truly trust in You.
Amen.

Tuesday of Holy Week

✢ Morning

Presence
Great Friend,
Peter was not the ideal apostle,
   just the usual.

Grace
Abba, give me Paul's mind but Peter's heart.

Psalm
Lady Wisdom has made her house ready,
roasted lamb, drawn wine, laid her table.
She's dismissed her servants and gone to the center of town.
"Anyone here confused?" she calls to those who'll listen.
"Anyone doubtful about which way to turn?
Come and have dinner with me! Puzzlement's fine!
Doubt keeps you from being stodgy, smug, secure.
Sit at my table and try to trip up the learned.
If you do and they're honest, they'll love you for it."
Wisdom comes slowly; cynicism is quick as poison.
Wisdom uplifts; the mocker is his own burden.
                   —Proverbs 9:1–12

Hymn
Grand is the seen, the light, to me—grand are the sky
      and stars,
Grand is the earth, and grand are lasting time and space,
And grand their laws, so multiform, puzzling,
      evolutionary;
But grander far the unseen soul of me, comprehending,
      endowing all those,

Lighting the light, the sky and stars, delving the earth,
      sailing the sea,
(What were all those, indeed, without thee, unseen soul?
      of what amount without thee?)
More evolutionary, vast, puzzling, O my soul!
More multiform far—more lasting thou than they.
—WALT WHITMAN, "GRAND IS THE SEEN"

Dedication
God, my Friend,
I offer You each moment of this day:
whatever comes—the unexpected challenges,
   diversions from my plans,
   the need-filled glance,
   the expectations and complaints,
   the being taken for granted,
   the slights and sleights-of-hand.
I'd be grateful if You could keep me aware of my pesky
      habits, like . . .
And, between us, perhaps we can enliven the spirits of
      those I live and work with, like . . .
Whatever else befalls,
   I trust we can cope with it,
   together.
Amen.

✠ Daytime

Presence
Great Friend,
we're so fearful of true passion,
   so afraid to "give ourselves away,"
   so afraid truly to live.

Grace
Abba, make me terrified only of mediocrity.

Psalm

Lord, You have seduced me, and I let myself be duped!
You're so strong, and I'm so weak. You overwhelmed me.
I've become a laughingstock, a fool for You!
I made up my mind. I will not even *think* of Him.
I *swear* I will not speak His name again!
But . . . but His words are burning in my belly,
sizzling through the marrow of my bones!
The effort to fight against Him has worn me out.
I *can't!* Oh, God, I simply can't be silent.

—JEREMIAH 20:7–9

Hymn

Peter,
Founder member of the Christian Church.
The Activist.
Always asking questions.

Bit like Corporal Jones, "I'd like to be the
First to volunteer, Sir!"
Unnerved by silence and the mystical.

He had to *do* something.

Walk on water,
Build three booths—"I don't know—
We can't just *sit* here, doing nothing!
Don't worry Sir, I'm right behind you.
No one'll touch you while I'm here."

And Jesus weighs him up and thinks, "Oh yes?"

Did he ever change?
He stayed with Jesus longer than the others.
And when at last he also ran away,
It seems he minded more than anyone.

No hero after all. Only human. Unreliable.
Not fit to be trusted.

"Simon Peter, do you love me?"

—ANN R. PARKER

Reading

A man is human, is alive according to what he has in common with other men. The somber man without his joys would not be a man, as neither would the joyful man without his somber moods. The weakness of the strong, the decisions of the indecisive, the brave sallies of the cowards, the cowardly moments of the valiant, the commonplaces of the geniuses and the aspirations of the simple, all of this, the intimate contradictions of men, is what makes them brothers.

—MIGUEL DE UNAMUNO

Scripture

It was night. When Judas had left, Jesus said: "Now's the time. The Son of Man has begun his journey to glory, to be seen for who I truly am. God will be glorified in me, and in turn He will glorify me within Himself. Little children, I have very little time left with you now. You will look for me but, as I told the priests, you can't come where I am going. But I'm leaving you a new commandment: love one another. Really, sincerely love one another in the same way I've loved you. That is the indelible sign that you belong to me, how outsiders will know you are mine: that you love one another." Simon Peter was always edgy dealing with matters beyond his understanding. "Lord," he said. "Please. *Where* are you going?" Jesus smiled at him fondly. "Right now, you can't follow me where I'm going." He patted Peter's hand. "But soon enough, you will." Peter was mildly indignant. "*Why* can't I follow you right now? I will lay down my *life* for you!" Jesus sighed. "Lay down your life for me? Ah, Peter. Believe me, before the cock crows tomorrow morning, you'll deny you even know me. Not just once. Three times."

—John 13:31–38

Closing
God, my Friend,
I *will* make mistakes.
But I *will* try.
Amen.

✿ Evening

Presence
Great Friend,
when I stumble, Your hand is there,
if only I'm humble enough to reach for it.

Grace
Abba, remind me that every night is only temporary.

Psalm 71
In You, Lord, I deposit all my weaknesses,
entrust them to Your justice and loving-kindness.
Be the stronghold that guards me from the shrewd,
and just as much a sentry against myself.
Since the safety of my mother's womb, You've been my
      refuge.
You've seen me through misery and hardship so many
      times,
and I know that now You'll lead me to life again.
I will sing Your praises even from the darkness.

Hymn
Come down, O Christ, and help me! reach Thy hand,
For I am drowning in a stormier sea

Than Simon on Thy lake of Galilee:
The wine of life is spilt upon the sand,
My heart is as some famine-murdered land
Whence all good things have perished utterly,
And well I know my soul in Hell must lie
If I this night before God's throne should stand.
"He sleeps perchance, or rideth to the chase,
Like Baal, when his prophets howled that name
From morn to noon on Carmel's smitten height."
Nay, peace, I shall behold before the night,
The feet of brass, the robe more white than flame,
The wounded hands, the weary human face.
—Oscar Wilde, *E Tenebris*

Closing
Holy Friend,
into Your hands, once again,
I commend my spirit.
Amen.

Spy Wednesday

✙ Morning

Presence
Great Friend,
this is the day of Judas.
A grim day.

Grace
Abba, help me always to know my place.

Psalm 41
My enemies whisper behind my back, "He's doomed.
When will he die and his name disappear from
      memory?"
They come at me and speak in hollow words,
then they leave and distort everything I've said.
They snicker over their plans to make me suffer.
Even my trusted friend, who shared the food at my table,
is ready to boot me down if I raise my head.
But, my God, when You raise me up, they'll see
that I've come through unscathed, renewed in the fire.

Hymn
Oh, opportunity! thy guilt is great,
'Tis thou that execut'st the traitor's treason;
Thou set'st the wolf where he the lamb may get;
Whoever plots the sin, thou point'st the season;
'Tis thou that spurn'st at right, at law, at reason;
And in thy shady cell, where none may spy him,
Sits Sin to seize the souls that wander by him.
      —WILLIAM SHAKESPEARE, *THE RAPE OF LUCRECE*

Dedication

God, my Friend,
I offer You each moment of this day:
whatever comes—the unexpected challenges,
    diversions from my plans,
    the need-filled glance,
    the expectations and complaints,
    the being taken for granted,
    the slights and sleights-of-hand.
I'd be grateful if You could keep me aware of my pesky
            habits, like . . .
And, between us, perhaps we can enliven the spirits of
            those I live and work with, like . . .
Whatever else befalls,
    I trust we can cope with it,
    together.
Amen.

✤ Daytime

Presence

Great Friend,
"love" is such a slippery label,
    and we misapply it so often.
I'd like to understand love better.

Grace

Abba, let my loving never mean control.

Psalm

When I assumed the task of shepherd from the money-
            hungry priests,
I had two staffs. One I called Goodwill, the other
            Harmony.

But the unruly sheep wore me out as had the unworthy
    shepherds.
So I broke my staff, Goodwill, like their covenant with
    God,
and I said to the owners, "Give me what's due me. Or
    not."
So they weighed out my wages, thirty shekels of silver,
no more than they'd have to pay to buy a slave.
But God said to me, "They insult both you and Me.
Take their paltry sum and throw it into the Temple."
So I did, and I broke my second staff called Harmony.
                    —ZECHARIAH 11:7–14

Hymn
Christ washed the feet of Judas!
The dark and evil passions of his soul,
His secret plot, and sordidness complete,
His hate, his purposing, Christ knew the whole,
And still in love he stooped and washed his feet.
Christ washed the feet of Judas!
Yet all his lurking sin was bare to him,
His bargain with the priest, and more than this,
In Olivet, beneath the moonlight dim,
Aforehand knew and felt his treacherous kiss.
Christ washed the feet of Judas!
And thus a girded servant, self-abased,
Taught that no wrong this side the gate of heaven
Was ever too great to wholly be effaced,
And though unasked, in spirit be forgiven.
And so if we have ever felt the wrong
Of Trampled rights, of caste, it matters not,
What e'er the soul has felt or suffered long,
Oh, heart! this one thing should not be forgot:
Christ washed the feet of Judas.
                —GEORGE MCCLELLAN, *THE FEET OF JUDAS*

Reading

The look on her face now was one I did not understand. I think a lover—I mean, a man who loved—might look so on a woman who had been false to him. And at last she said, "You are indeed teaching me about kinds of love I did not know. It is like looking into a deep pit. I am not sure whether I like your kind better than hatred. Oh, Orual—to take my love for you, because you know it goes down to my very roots and cannot be diminished by any other newer love, and then to make of it a tool, a weapon, a thing of policy and mastery, an instrument of torture—I begin to think I never knew you. Whatever comes, something that was between us dies here."

—C. S. Lewis, *Till We Have Faces*

Scripture

One of the Twelve, Judas Iscariot, went to the chief priests and said, "All right. What will you give me if I hand him over to you?" They tried to contain their delight at this opportunity—and their disdain. They gave him thirty pieces of silver, the price for a decent slave. From then on, Judas kept his eyes peeled for a chance to arrest Jesus without causing a riot. Contrary to custom, Jesus decided to celebrate the feast with his friends a day earlier. He told them to go to a man in the city and say, "The Master says, 'My time is near. I need to borrow your house to celebrate Passover with my disciples.'" And his people did as he told them. When evening came and he was seated with the Twelve, he said, "I have to tell you the bare truth. One of you is going to betray me." There was consternation, each one in turn saying, "Surely not me" and "You can't possibly think. . . . " Jesus said very calmly, "Someone who has shared this dish with me will betray me. The Son of Man is ready for his fate, as the scriptures foretold. But what a sad fate for the one who gives him away. Better if he'd never been born." Judas asked, coldly, "Master, surely not me?" Jesus nodded. "As you say."

—Matthew 26:14–25

Closing
God, my Friend,
for all my betrayals in the past,
again, I ask Your forgiveness.
Amen.

✦ Evening

Presence
Great Friend,
Your Son, our Brother,
died so that sins could be *forgiven*.

Grace
Abba, make me a channel of Your peace.

Psalm
We had all wandered off, like mindless sheep.
But God took all our rebelliousness and laid it on him.
Beaten and tortured, he never said a word,
like a lamb led in our place to the slaughterhouse.
After his unjust sentence, he was taken away.
And did anyone standing aloof even care?
That he went to his death without a thought for himself?
That he was the scapegoat for all our thoughtless
        defiance?
But after his ordeal, he will enter the light, vindicated.
                        —Isaiah 53:6–8, 11

Hymn
God of our weary years,
God of our silent tears,
Thou who hast brought us thus far on the way;
Thou who hast by Thy might
Led us into light,
Keep us forever in the path, we pray.
Lest our feet stray from the places, our God, where we
        met Thee,

Lest, our hearts drunk with the wine of the world, we
        forget Thee,
Shadowed beneath Thy hand,
May we forever stand.
True to our God,
True to our native land.
            —James Weldon Johnson, "Lift Every Voice and Sing"

Closing
Holy Friend,
help my soul
absorb all this week means.
Amen.

Holy Thursday

✣ Morning

Presence
Great Friend,
as I ponder the people
    with whom I live and work,
I wonder,
    whose feet would I dread to wash?

Grace
Abba, make me proud to be a servant.

Psalm
During the Passover supper, knowing his Father
had now put everything into his hands,
Jesus rose from the table and took off his outer garments.
He tied a towel round his waist and knelt before them.
He moved from one to the next with a basin of water,
washing each one's feet and drying them with the towel.
When he'd finished, he said. "Now you are clean. But
        not all.
Do you understand what I've just done for you?
You call me 'teacher' and 'master,' and so I am.
But if I, the teacher and master, have washed your feet,
then you, too, should wash one another's feet.
What I've done for you, you must do for one another."
                                    —JOHN 13:1–5, 10–15

Hymn
Go, labor on; spend, and be spent;
Thy joy to do the Father's will;

It is the way the Master went;
Should not the servant tread it still?

Go, labor on: 'tis not for nought;
Thy earthly loss is heav'nly gain;
Men heed thee, love thee, praise thee not;
The Master praises, what are men?

Press on, faint not, keep watch and pray;
Be wise the erring soul to win;
Go forth into the world's highway,
Compel the wanderer to come in.

Press on, and in thy work rejoice;
For work comes rest, the prize thus won;
Soon shalt thou hear the Master's voice,
The midnight cry, Behold, I come!
　　　　—HORATIUS BONAR, SONGS FOR THE WILDERNESS (1843)

Dedication
God, my Friend,
I offer You each moment of this day:
whatever comes—the unexpected challenges,
　　diversions from my plans,
　　the need-filled glance,
　　the expectations and complaints,
　　the being taken for granted,
　　the slights and sleights-of-hand.
I'd be grateful if You could keep me aware of my pesky
　　　　habits, like . . .
And, between us, perhaps we can enliven the spirits of
　　　　those I live and work with, like . . .
Whatever else befalls,
　　I trust we can cope with it,
　　together.
Amen.

✝ Daytime

Presence
Great Friend,
I never want the Eucharist
   to become commonplace
   and not an astounding event, each time.

Grace
Abba, keep me amazed at this wondrous Gift.

Psalm
The Lord said, "Let this be the first month of your year.
On the tenth day, every family must procure its lamb,
a year-old unblemished male, sheep or goat.
On the fourteenth day, slaughter the lambs at twilight.
Daub their blood on each doorpost and lintel,
and that same night roast and eat its flesh
with unleavened bread and bitter herbs.
Eat it dressed for travel, staff in hand.
This night is the Passover of the Lord!
I will pass through Egypt slaying every firstborn,
human or beast, in judgment of their pagan gods.
But I will bypass every door splashed with the sacrifice.
This night is the Passover of the Lord!"

—Exodus 12:1–8, 11–14

Hymn

Panis Angelicus fit panis hominum;
Dat panis coelicus figuris terminum:
O res mirabilis! Manducat Dominum.
Pauper, pauper, servus et humilis.

Angels' Bread is now human bread!
Heavenly Bread ends mere symbols.
How wondrous! The poor, poor humble servant feeds on the Lord!

Te trina Deitas, unaque poscimus,	Mighty God, One-in-Three, we beg
Sic nos tu visita, sicut te colimus;	You to visit us, as we adore You,
Per tuas semitas duc nos quo tendimus,	and lead us by your paths where you will
Ad lucem quam inhabitas.	to the light in which You dwell.

—MUSIC BY CESAR FRANCK, TRANSLATION MINE

Reading

"How can He put on," [mad Malle] said, "such a home-spun coat, and not burn all up with the touch of Him? If He shouldered down the sun, and quenched light with His coming, it would be no marvel." Wat scrambled up, and catching a handful of her gown shook it impatiently, being hungry. Malle shoved into his hands two thick slabs of bread with lard between, and he went back to the hearth. But she lingered at the table. "Instead," she murmured, "He came stilly as rain, and even now cometh into the darkness of our bellies—God in a bit of bread, to bring morning to our souls. *There* is news."

—H. F. M. PRESCOTT, *THE MAN ON A DONKEY*

Scripture

While they were eating the Passover meal, Jesus took bread into his hands, said the blessing over it, and gave it to his friends. "Take this, and eat it," he said. "This is my body." Then he took a cup of wine, gave thanks again and handed it round, saying, "Drink from this, all of you. This is my blood, the blood sealing the new covenant between God and all humankind. It will be freely poured out, so that sins may be forgiven. From this moment, I shall never drink wine again until I drink new wine with you in my Father's kingdom."

—MATTHEW 26:26–29

Closing

God, my Friend,
I'm not worthy
    that You enter me, body and soul.
But only say the word,
    and I shall be made worthy.
Amen.

✟ Evening

Presence

Great Friend,
tonight is the *kairos*:
    the appointed time.

Grace

Abba, let me remember the price at which my soul was bought.

Psalm

After the meal, they walked to the Mount of Olives,
a quiet grove where Jesus often prayed alone.
He said to his people, "Watch and pray, to face this test."
He withdrew a bit and knelt to pray: "Father!
If You are willing, oh, *please* take this cup from me!
But if not, Your will be done, not mine."
He felt a messenger from God, consoling, fortifying him.
Still, he prayed in anguish so deep his sweat was like blood.
Then he rose and found his disciples asleep, exhausted.
"Why are you asleep. Wake up and pray for courage."
Suddenly, while he was still speaking, soldiers appeared
with Judas leading them, aware of this secret place.
Judas approached to kiss him to single him out.
Jesus smiled. "Judas, you betray your Lord with a kiss?"
His terrified friends said, "Lord, shall we fight them?"
and one of them struck a guard and clipped off his right ear.

Jesus said, "Enough!" and touched the ear and healed it.
Then he said to the captains and the Temple chaplains,
"So. Am I a bandit that you come for me with swords?
When I taught in public, you never laid a hand on me.
But this is the time. This is the reign of darkness."

—LUKE 22:39–53

Hymn
Thou that on sin's wages starvest,
Behold we have the joy in harvest:
For us was gather'd the first-fruits,
For us was lifted from the roots,
Sheaved in cruel bands, bruised sore,
Scourged upon the threshing-floor;
Where the upper mill-stone roof'd His head,
At morn we found the heavenly Bread,
And, on a thousand altars laid,
Christ our Sacrifice is made!

Thou whose dry plot for moisture gapes,
We shout with them that tread the grapes:
For us the Vine was fenced with thorn,
Five ways the precious branches torn;
Terrible fruit was on the tree
In the acre of Gethsemane;
For us by Calvary's distress
The wine was racked from the press;
Now in our altar-vessels stored
Is the sweet Vintage of Our Lord.

—GERARD MANLEY HOPKINS, S.J., "BARNFLOOR AND WINEPRESS"

Closing
Holy Friend,
at last the serpent's false promise
    is fulfilled:
"Eat this,
    and you'll become like God."
Amen.

Good Friday

✦ Morning

Presence
Great Friend,
this is the day
when ultimate Love shows itself.

Grace
Abba, remind me how true conquest can arise from impotence.

Psalm
The chief priests and all the worthy elders assembled,
trying to find evidence to have Jesus executed,
but they kept coming up empty-handed.
Witnesses gave false testimony, a conflicting hodge-
      podge.
Some said, "He claimed he was going to destroy the
      Temple!
And rebuild it in three days! With no hands!"
Finally, in frustration, the high priest pulled Jesus to his
      face.
"Well? Have you *nothing* to say of the evidence against
      you?"
But Jesus was silent and gave them no answer at all.
Finally, his face ferocious, the high priest shouted:
"*Are* you the Christ, the Son of the living God?"
Quietly, resolutely, Jesus said, "I AM!
And you will see me seated at God's right hand in
      heaven."
Apoplectic, the high priest ripped his tunic in horror.
"Enough! What need have we for witnesses?

Blasphemy! What is your decision, my brothers?"
Unanimously, they declared he deserved to die.
Some of the elders came up to spit in his face,
slapping him and saying, "Play the prophet now!"

—MARK 14:55–65

Hymn
One crown that no one seeks
And yet the highest head
Its isolation coveted
Its stigma deified

While Pontius Pilate lives
In whatsoever hell
That coronation pierces him
He recollects it well.

—EMILY DICKINSON

Dedication
God, my Friend,
I offer You each moment of this day:
whatever comes—the unexpected challenges,
    diversions from my plans,
    the need-filled glance,
    the expectations and complaints,
    the being taken for granted,
    the slights and sleights-of-hand.
I'd be grateful if You could keep me aware of my pesky
        habits, like . . .
And, between us, perhaps we can enliven the spirits of
        those I live and work with, like . . .
Whatever else befalls,
    I trust we can cope with it,
    together.
Amen.

✤ Daytime

Presence
Great Friend,
Your Son came
to show us how it's done.

Grace
Abba, whenever I suffer unjustly—and I will—make me remember this day.

Psalm
"My people, My people! What have I *done* to you?
How have I disappointed you? Answer Me, *answer* Me!"
—Micah 6:3

Hymn
Were you there when they crucified my Lord?
Were you there when they crucified my Lord?
Oh, sometimes it causes me to tremble, tremble, tremble.
Were you there when they crucified my Lord?

Were you there when they nailed him to the tree?
Were you there when they nailed him to the tree?
Oh, sometimes it causes me to tremble, tremble, tremble.
Were you there when they nailed him to the tree?

Were you there when they laid him in the tomb?
Were you there when they laid him in the tomb?
Oh, sometimes it causes me to tremble, tremble, tremble.
Were you there when they laid him in the tomb?

Reading
I find it difficult to imagine the "holy-card" Jesus—pale, spindly, ethereal—like no other outdoor carpenter I've ever

seen—enduring the Passion described by the gospels. He was scourged—chained to a pillar while two husky guardsmen lashed him with thongs embedded with lumps of lead, back, shoulders, thighs, calves, loins, laying open the flesh so the bone shows white in the crimson meat. His head whirls with giddiness and nausea. Then with pliers, they braid a crown of thorns and beat them into his head, through the scalp to the skull, blood running down into his tangled hair and beard. Then they put on his tunic and yoke the crosspiece (about the size and weight of a railroad tie) to his raw shoulders and boot him outside toward the Ephraim gate. But he falls and faints too often, the burden cracking down on him, so they enlist Simon of Cyrene to carry it. Otherwise, he won't last. They climb the hill and stop, stripping his homespun tunic which has begun to adhere to the flesh like a bandage. They stretch him with the raw meat of his back in the gravel and spike him at the wrists to the crossbar. A trail of fire bursts up his arms into his brain. They get him on his feet and back him toward the upright, pulleying him up so his ravaged back inches up the raw wood. They flatten his feet against the upright and, with a few vigorous hammer-blows, spike his ankles.

He has had nothing to eat or drink in about eighteen hours. The loss of blood has left him gasping, unable to swallow his own saliva. Some simpleton soldier offers him sour wine, knowing it often brings on a fatal fainting fit. But Jesus refuses. All the muscles of his body begin to cramp and contract. He gasps for air, like an asthmatic. He is asphyxiating. Whenever he chooses to speak, he must lift himself up, pressing against his pinioned feet. And he lasted for at least three hours. He was not the "holy-card" Jesus.

—SEE DR. PIERRE BARBET, *A DOCTOR AT CALVARY*

Scripture

When they reached the place called Skull, they crucified him with two criminals, one on his right, the other on his left. Jesus groaned, "Father, forgive them! They don't know what they're doing." Then the soldiers threw dice to divide his meager clothing. A crowd stood around, gaping. The priests hooted: "Ha-*ha!* He saved others! Now let this Christ, this Chosen One rescue *himself!*" He hung there under a sign, "This is the King of the Jews," so the soldiers mocked him, too, offering him vinegar to drink, saying, "If you *are* King of the Jews, Big Man, save yourself!" One of the dying criminals joined in the abuse. "If you're the Christ, save your ass. Save ours, too, while you're at it!" But the other spoke up angrily, "Don't you fear God at all? We got the same sentence he did. But we deserve it! But this man's done *nothing* wrong." He turned to Jesus and muttered, "Jesus, when you come into this kingdom of yours, please remember me." Jesus raised his head and almost smiled. "My friend, I promise you that today you'll be with me in paradise." It was now mid-afternoon, and the sun's light dimmed so that for hours the world was in darkness. The veil of the inner Temple sanctuary ripped right down the middle. At that moment, Jesus raised his parched voice and shouted, "Father, into your hands I commit my spirit." And he breathed his last.

—LUKE 23:33–46

Closing
God, my Friend,
into Your hands
   I commend my spirit.
Amen.

✤ Evening

Presence
Great Friend,
not Abraham, nor even Job,
trusted as He did
that You truly love Him.

Grace
Abba, I am not the worst of sinners, but remind me that I am a sinner.

Psalm 22
My God, my God! Why have You abandoned me?
My strength is trickling away, my bones disjointed.
My heart is melting inside my chest like wax.
My mouth is as parched as a shard of earthenware.
My tongue cleaves to the roof of my mouth,
as they stretch me out in the dirt to kill me.
A gang of villains, like a pack of wild dogs,
circles me to fang my hands and my feet.
"He trusted himself to God. Let God help him now!"
I can count every bone as they look on and gloat.
They cast lots for my clothes to divide among them.
God, don't remain aloof. Don't let this last forever.
No matter what, I will praise You to the bitter end.

Hymn
If on these things I durst not looke, durst I
Upon his miserable mother cast mine eye,
Who was God's partner here, and furnished thus,
Halfe of that Sacrifice, which ransomed us?
Though these things, as I ride, be from mine eye,
They'are present yet unto my memory,
For that looks towards them; and thou look'st towards
         me,
O Saviour, as thou hang'st upon the tree;
I turne my backe to thee, but to receive,
Corrections, till thy mercies bid thee leave.
O thinke mee worth thine anger, punish mee.
Burne off my rusts, and my deformity,
Restore thine Image, so much, by thy grace,
That thou may'st know mee, and I'll turne my face.
                        —JOHN DONNE, *GOOD FRIDAY, 1613*

Closing
Holy Friend,
I trust that, from the abyss,
there is only one way:
    upward.
Amen.

Holy Saturday

⊕ Morning

Presence
Great Friend,
this is the loneliest of days,
when Life seems to have deserted the world.

Grace
Abba, without Your sustenance, all life would cease.

Psalm 31
In You, O Lord, I have taken refuge.
May my abasement not last forever.
To all my foes, I'm an object of reproach.
Even my friends deny they know me
and run from any suggestion of my name.
I'm like a broken dish, discarded, useless,
as forgotten as the unremembered dead.
But I trust in You, Lord. You are my God.

Hymn
The time you won your town the race
We chaired you through the market-place;
Man and boy stood cheering by,
And home we brought you shoulder-high.
To-day, the road all runners come,
Shoulder-high we bring you home,
And set you at your threshold down,
Townsman of a stiller town.
                    —A. E. HOUSMAN, "TO AN ATHLETE DYING YOUNG"

Dedication

God, my Friend,
I offer You each moment of this day:
whatever comes—the unexpected challenges,
    diversions from my plans,
    the need-filled glance,
    the expectations and complaints,
    the being taken for granted,
    the slights and sleights-of-hand.
I'd be grateful if You could keep me aware of my pesky
        habits, like . . .
And, between us, perhaps we can enliven the spirits of
        those I live and work with, like . . .
Whatever else befalls,
    I trust we can cope with it,
      together.
Amen.

✚ Daytime

Presence

Great Friend,
with infinite patience,
You evolved us from the laval swamp—
    to live, to feel, to reason.
And now, You invite us to evolve
    into Your divine life.

Grace

Abba, help me to carry this ennobling with good grace.

Psalm

In the days when Christ shared the burdens of the flesh,
he offered prayers with loud cries and tears
to the One who could save him from suffering death.

And he was heard, not saved from death but from death
      after dying,
since dying for our sake was the whole purpose of his life.
Son though he was, he learned obedience through
      submission,
so that when he triumphed he became a source of life for
      all.

                       —HEBREWS 5:7–10

Hymn

Sleep, sleep, old sun, thou canst not have repass'd,
As yet, the wound thou took'st on Friday last;
Sleep then, and rest; the world may bear thy stay;
A better sun rose before thee to-day;
Who—not content to enlighten all that dwell
On the earth's face, as thou—enlighten'd hell,
And made the dark fires languish in that vale,
As at thy presence here our fires grow pale;
Whose body, having walk'd on earth, and now
Hasting to heaven, would—that He might allow
Himself unto all stations, and fill all—
For these three days become a mineral.
He was all gold when He lay down, but rose
All tincture, and doth not alone dispose
Leaden and iron wills to good, but is
Of power to make e'en sinful flesh like his.
Had one of those, whose credulous piety
Thought that a soul one might discern and see
Go from a body, at this sepulchre been,
And, issuing from the sheet, this body seen,
He would have justly thought this body a soul,
If not of any man, yet of the whole.

          —JOHN DONNE, *RESURRECTION, IMPERFECT*

Reading

Those who spread their sails in the right way to the winds of the earth will always find themselves borne by a current towards the open seas. The more nobly a person wills and acts, the more avid they become for great and sublime aims to pursue. They will no longer be content with family, country, and the remunerative aspect of their work. They will want wider organizations to create, new paths to blaze, causes to uphold, truths to discover, an ideal to cherish and defend. So, gradually, they no longer belong to themselves. Little by little the great breath of the universe has insinuated itself into them through the fissure of their humble but faithful action, and has broadened them, and raised them up, borne them on.

—PIERRE TEILHARD DE CHARDIN, *THE DIVINE MILIEU*

Scripture

When it was all over, Joseph of Arimathea, a disciple of Jesus secretly because of fear of the priests, asked Pilate if he could remove the body of Jesus, and Pilate allowed it. So he came and took the corpse. Nicodemus, another secret believer who had come to Jesus only at night, brought a large amount of aromatic spices, and they took the body of Jesus and bound it with the spices in burial cloths, as was the custom. Near the place where he had been crucified, there was a garden and in it a newly hewn tomb in which no one had ever been laid. So they laid the body of Jesus inside and then went quickly home.

—JOHN 19:38–42

Closing

God, my Friend,
what a grace!
To know how the Story ends!
Amen.

✚ Evening

Presence
Great Friend,
in the silence of that tomb,
a whole new world was coming to birth.

Grace
Abba, let Your new aliveness within me be obvious.

Psalm
While I was watching, thrones were set in place,
and the Most Venerable took His exalted seat.
His robe was white like crystal hoarfrost,
His hair like a silver cloud of wool.
His throne was a chalice of flame pouring from His
       presence.
A thousand thousand bowed before His glory,
and the books lay open in which all human deeds were
       written.
In the vision, I saw the Representative of all things
       human
coming on the clouds of heaven into the Sacred
       Presence.
On Him was bestowed the power to rule all things,
all people, all colors, all languages, all ways of thought.
His rule is everlasting, and His Kingdom shall have no end.
       —Daniel 7:9–10, 13–14

Hymn
On a rusty iron throne
Past the furthest star of space
I saw Satan sit alone,
Old and haggard was his face;
For his work was done and he
Rested in eternity.

And to him from out the sun
Came his father and his friend
Saying, now the work is done
Enmity is at an end:
And he guided Satan to
Paradises that he knew.

Gabriel without a frown,
Uriel without a spear,
Raphael came singing down
Welcoming their ancient peer,
And they seated him beside
One who had been crucified.

—JAMES STEPHENS (B. 1882)

Closing
Holy Friend,
insofar as I am able,
I am ready to serve.
Amen.

Easter Sunday

♱ Morning

Presence
Great Friend,
today is the bedrock
of all I believe about life.

Grace
Abba, remind me that all I do now echoes into eternity.

Psalm
If Christ was raised out of death, how can you doubt *your*
     rising?
And if Christ was not raised, the core of all we believe is
     hollow.
Your faith is pointless, self-delusive, if his rising is not a
     fact.
Then all who have fallen asleep, believing, are utterly lost.
If Christ's life is merely an inspiration for how to live,
and then we walk through the door of death to oblivion,
then we are the most pitiable fools on the face of the
     earth.
                          —1 Corinthians 15:12–19

Hymn
He is arisen! Glorious word!
Now reconciled is God, my Lord;
The gates of heaven are open.
My Jesus did triumphant die,
And Satan's arrows broken lie,
Destroyed hell's direst weapon.
Oh, hear

What cheer!
Christ victorious
Riseth glorious,
Life He giveth
He was dead, but see, He liveth!

—BIRGITTE K. BOYE

Dedication
God, my Friend,
I offer You each moment of this day:
whatever comes—the unexpected challenges,
    diversions from my plans,
    the need-filled glance,
    the expectations and complaints,
    the being taken for granted,
    the slights and sleights-of-hand.
I'd be grateful if You could keep me aware of my pesky
        habits, like . . .
And, between us, perhaps we can enliven the spirits of
        those I live and work with, like . . .
Whatever else befalls,
    I trust we can cope with it,
    together.
Amen.

✟ Daytime

Presence
Great Friend,
how could we ever doubt our value
when we've been welcomed
at such a Price?

Grace
Abba, help me open my heart and soul to this greatness
You offer.

Psalm

He is the embodiment of the invisible God,
the model of all that creation has been reaching for.
In him, all things in heaven and on earth were created—
everything visible and invisible—all life, all goodness, all
    love.
He exists before all-that-is could possibly exist,
and he is the force in whom things hold together.
He is the head of the Church, his living body on earth
and in heaven: the beginning, the first born from the
    dead,
so that he will be supreme, filling the gaps in all that is,
bringing peace and reconciliation of all creation to its
    Creator—
amnesty and unconditional forgiveness through his
    death.

—COLOSSIANS 1:15–20

Hymn

The kingdom of this world is become
the Kingdom of our Lord and of His Christ, and of His
    Christ;
and He shall reign for ever and ever
King of Kings,
for ever and ever. Hallelujah! Hallelujah!
and Lord of Lords,
for ever and ever. Hallelujah! Hallelujah!

And He shall reign for ever and ever,
for ever and ever,
King of Kings,
and Lord of Lords,
King of Kings,
and Lord of Lords,
and He shall reign for ever and ever,

King of Kings,
and Lord of Lords.
Hallelujah! Hallelujah! Hallelujah! Hallelujah!
    Hallelujah!

—GEORG FRIEDRICH HANDEL

Reading

No one saw it happen. The early writers are very forth-right about that. If they had wanted, they could have sketched a real Spielberg scene: "The rocks seemed almost 'uneasy,' trembling. Then they began to shimmer and quake, etc., etc." But they were honest enough not to. All we have is the testimony of people who claimed to have encountered him alive after he had been demonstrably dead. What's more, they went to often horrifying deaths rather than deny that experience of Jesus risen. All they had to do was say, "We were fooled. We made it all up to get a fol-lowing." But they didn't. Something earthshaking had hap-pened to them. That's undeniable. Good Friday, they cow-ered like rats behind the locked doors of the upper room. Then, in little more than a month, those same despicable turncoats were out on the streets! Preaching fearlessly of their experience. Daring imprisonment, ostracism, rejec-tion from the Temple that had been the focus of their lives. Because they claimed to have experienced the inconceiv-able: a man come back from the dead. Every one of their martyrdoms was a death-bed confession to that experience. I tend to believe those.

Scripture

[Mary Magdalene had come to the tomb where they had laid Jesus and, to her astonishment, it was empty. She had run to the disciples, still hiding, and Peter and John had run to the tomb themselves and found that, even though the news was unthinkable, it was true.] Mary returned and stood at the open cave, weeping. But when she stooped to look inside again, she saw two blinding presences sitting where the corpse had been, one at the head, one at the foot. "Lady," they said quietly, "why are you weeping?" And she mumbled in terror, "They've taken my Lord away, and I don't know where they've put him!" As she turned away, she saw a man standing there, not realizing it was Jesus, presuming it was the gardener. "Why are you weeping?" Jesus said. "You are looking for someone?" She said, "Oh, sir, *please!* If you know where they've taken him, *tell* me, and I'll go to him." The man smiled. "Mary," he said. She squinted again at him and fell to grasp his knees. "*Rabboni,*" she gasped. Gently, Jesus raised her to her feet. "Don't cling to me. I've not yet risen to my Father. But go tell the brothers I am ascending to my Father—who is now truly your Father, too, and your God." So Mary, no matter what she had been, was the first eyewitness to bring news to the others.

—John 20:11–18

Closing
God, my Friend,
when Christ came back,
   no one recognized Him at first.
That should be a cautionary lesson
   about who might
   present Him to me.
Amen.

✛ Evening

Presence
Great Friend,
whatever evil we find
is Your invitation
to become alchemists.

Grace

Abba, whenever I am downcast, remind me what I've forgotten.

Psalm

The dead will be raised, imperishable, and our mortal
      nature
will be fused into immortality. Then scripture is fulfilled:
Death is swallowed up forever in victory!
Death, where is your triumph? Where is your sting?
The sting of death lies in death as loss and separation,
in our fear that sinners can't possibly *merit* God's love.
But Christ *gives* us forgiveness, and value, and eternal
      life!
Therefore, dear friends, keep firm and unshakable,
alive with the energy of Christ for his ongoing work.
And in the Lord Christ, none of your labors—none—is
      wasted!

—Romans 15:54–58

Hymn

In the resurrection morning,
Blessed thought it is to me,
We shall rise (Hallelujah!), we shall rise!
I shall see my blessed Savior, who so freely died for me,
We shall rise, (Hallelujah!) we shall rise (in that morning
      we shall rise).

In the resurrection morning,
We shall meet Him in the air,
We shall rise (Hallelujah!),
And be carried up to glory, To our home so bright and
      fair,
We shall rise, (Hallelujah!) we shall rise (in that morning
      we shall rise).

Closing
Holy Friend,
the end
is the beginning.
Amen.

Credits

The author and publisher have endeavored to credit all known persons holding copyright or reproduction rights for passages quoted in this book and gratefully acknowledge the following: